Brain Matters:
The Missing Link

*Releasing the
Hidden Healing Power
of Your Brain*

Dr. Joseph F. Unger, Jr

CAVU Concepts, LLC

Brain Matters: The Missing Link
Releasing the Hidden Power of Your Brain
Dr. Joseph F. Unger, Jr., DC, FICS

CAVU Concepts, LLC
Published by CAVU Concepts, LLC, St. Louis, MO
Copyright ©2019 Dr. Joseph F. Unger, Jr.
All rights reserved.

Limit of Liability/Disclaimer of Warranty: While the publisher and author have used their best efforts in preparing this book, they make no representations or warranties with respect to the accuracy or completeness of the contents of this book and specifically disclaim any implied warranties of merchantability or fitness for a particular purpose. No warranty may be created or extended by sales representatives or written sales materials. The advice and strategies contained herein may not be suitable for your situation. You should consult with a professional where appropriate. Neither the publisher nor author shall be liable for any loss of profit or any other commercial damages, including but not limited to special, incidental, consequential, or other damages.

Editor: Cheryl Roberts

Cover design: Jean Lopez

Illustrations: Laurie O'Keefe, Medical Illustrator

Interior design: Davis Creative, DavisCreative.com

Library of Congress Cataloging-in-Publication Data
Library of Congress Control Number: 2019915980
Dr. Joseph F. Unger, Jr.
Brain Matters: The Missing Link: Releasing the Hidden Power of Your Brain
ISBN: 978-09786711-3-6 (paperback)
     978-09786711-4-3 (ebook)
Library of Congress subject headings:
  1.   HEA000000 HEALTH & FITNESS / General 2. SEL000000 SELF-HELP / General 3. MED013000 MEDICAL / Chiropractic
2019

ATTENTION CORPORATIONS, UNIVERSITIES, COLLEGES AND PROFESSIONAL ORGANIZATIONS: Quantity discounts are available on bulk purchases of this book for educational, gift purposes, or as premiums for increasing magazine subscriptions or renewals. Special books or book excerpts can also be created to fit specific needs. For information, please contact CAVU Concepts, LLC. at http://www. BrainMattersTheMissingLink.com

Dedication

To my wife Cindy without whom this book might never have been written.

Acknowledgements

Rarely are books written in a vacuum. This one is no exception.

I owe a debt of thanks to so many:

- Those who see hope beyond the hopeless circumstances that have befallen them.
- Those who seek answers when everyone has told them there are none.
- Those who will stop at nothing to achieve their goals, to attain their dreams and to uncover the mysteries that plague humanity.
- All my patients, colleagues and teachers, each of whom have contributed, in their own unique way, to my understanding of the human condition as well as how to provide better understanding to a suffering humanity.

I must also thank, recognize and express appreciation for all those who have taught, inspired and motivated me over my entire life. They are too numerous to name individually because my gratitude extends to include friends, lecturers, books, audio tapes, television programs, radio interviews and more. In other words, it's a nearly endless list that would fill another book!

Two people I could never have done this without are my parents, Doris and Joseph. They instilled in me the perseverance to push forward, the curiosity to explore and the audacity to color outside the lines.

A special thank you goes to my wife, Cindy. Her steadfast support of this project extends back to the original idea to write this book. Her inspiration and conviction are the catalysts that got this project off the ground.

Her innumerable draft readings and gentle edits have helped make this book what it is today.

"Until one is committed, there is hesitancy, the chance to draw back. Concerning all acts of initiative (and creation), there is one elementary truth, the ignorance of which kills countless ideas and splendid plans: that the moment one definitely commits oneself, then Providence moves too. All sorts of things occur to help one that would never otherwise have occurred. A whole stream of events issues from the decision, raising in one's favor all manner of unforeseen incidents and meetings and material assistance, which no man could have dreamed would have come his way. Whatever you can do, or dream you can do, begin it. Boldness has genius, power, and magic in it. Begin it now."

– William H. Murray

Preface

Degenerative Brain Diseases – The Missing Link

This book is for anyone interested in gaining a better understanding of the mechanisms of our brains, and especially, what happens when our brains are not functioning as they were meant to.

Traumatic brain injury, Parkinson's disease, Alzheimer's, multiple sclerosis, dementia and other neurodegenerative diseases all involve loss of certain brain functions. What do they all have in common: the brain is not maintaining its optimal health and repair mechanisms.

Many treatment strategies address nutrition, diet, exercise and other therapeutic modalities. None to date have focused upon the innate healing mechanism of the brain, which involves cerebral spinal fluid flow and cranial function.

We have approximately 85 billion nerve cells in the brain and a nearly equal number of glial cells that surround and insulate neurons. Blood flow, lymphatic flow, Cerebral Spinal Fluid (CSF) flow and glial cells support function of the neurons providing nutrition and extracting waste materials. The cranial mechanisms described in **Brain Matters – The Missing Link** cannot be addressed by any means other than cranial manipulation.

Not only are the innate cranial mechanisms essential for normal health, healing and maintenance of the brain, they also affect pressures inside the head. If the cranial mechanism is not adequately pumping CSF down the spine, back pressure occurs. Such pressures run the risk of causing microscopic fractures in the Blood Brain Barrier (BBB). The brain is sheltered from the rest of the body by this barrier and is extremely sensitive to foreign materials breaching this essential, protective mechanism. This includes substances that are perfectly normal in the rest of the body. Even tiny amounts of leakage into the brain can trigger inflammatory buildup in the brain resulting in even more pressure. Certain materials entering the brain through these fissures also initiate autoimmune and possibly other negative reactions. Persons suffering from any of these conditions can benefit greatly from diet, nutrition, herbs, homeopathic remedies and numerous forms of brain training exercises. Some of the most complete and thorough sources of these interventions are as follows:

Why Isn't My Brain Working?
by Datis Kharrazian, PhD, DHSc, DC, MS, MMSc, FACN

Saving Your Brain
By Dr. Kelly Miller

For cutting-edge neurological training information and practitioners see:

Carrick Institute for Clinical Neuroscience and Rehabilitation
www.carrickinstitute.com

I am honored to present this book, **Brain Matters–The Missing Link**, as an addition to other important resources for brain healing. **Brain Matters–The Missing Link** provides an understanding of brain healing and therapeutic strategies that are not addressed by any other current authorities. This book primarily describes the healing potential of Chiropractic Craniopathy with a brief introduction to one energy therapy, the AlphaBio Centrix system of healing energetic patches. It is included in this manuscript due to its proven clinical effectiveness and the unique offering it provides.

Overview of *Brain Matters–The Missing Link: Releasing the Hidden Healing Power of Your Brain*

The Philosophy, Art and Science of cranial bone manipulation is 95 years old at this writing. Some philosophical constructs are over 200 years old and other cranial constructs were mentioned by Hippocrates, the Father of Medicine, over 2000 years ago.

Optimally, cranial bones move throughout life and pump cerebral spinal fluid throughout the entire central nervous system. This flow of cerebral spinal fluid (CSF) is an essential ingredient for health and healing. All variations of treatment and philosophy utilizing this mechanism (cranial manipulation), maintain the same fundamental construct, however, the treatment protocols and procedures are quite varied. They are also thoroughly confused by the general public, as well as by most professionals.

As a dedicated student to the subject matter for almost 45 years, I have scrutinized, teased out and clarified the subject matter in order to achieve a unique understanding and perspective. This book is aimed at the general public; however, because of the clarity of understanding that is afforded, it is equally applicable to professionals of all levels, from massage therapists to medical doctors, osteopaths and chiropractic physicians.

One historical correction and key points to be emphasized in the book:

The importance of cranial function in human beings and its relationship to health and healing were first postulated in the 1700s by Emmanuel Swedenborg. William Garner Sutherland (1873-1954), an osteopath, is usually attributed to the founding of the theories governing the cranial mechanisms. *This is untrue.* Dr. Sutherland used the constructs of Swedenborg without ever giving due credit.

In the 1920s and 30s, Dr. Nephi Cottam, a chiropractor, researched and published the first written materials concerning cranial manipulation. This publication predated Sutherland and largely goes unrecognized. Cottam also published the first book on cranial therapies and coined the term "Craniopathy." Sutherland referred to his therapies as "cranial osteopathy."

In later years, John Upledger, an osteopath, developed a format and style of cranial osteopathy that he termed "cranial sacral therapy".

Another chiropractor, Dr. Major Bertrand De Jarnette, developed an understanding of physical medicine that he termed the Sacro Occipital Technic™ (SOT®) Methods of chiropractic and Chiropractic Craniopathy. In more than 130 books, as well as thousands of research papers, Dr. De Jarnette integrated an understanding of the spine, pelvis, organ function—virtually the entire human mechanism in health and disease, that included cranial bones and their essential functions. De Jarnette embraced all the previous understanding of cranial therapies and developed a collection of different, unique and revolutionary insights and treatments.

One intention of this book is to describe the mechanisms and interventions that De Jarnette termed the cranial sutural procedures that, in this book, are referred to as the Integrated Sutural Protocols (ISP). **Brain Matters–The Missing Link** describes the anatomy, physiology and mechanics of the mechanism and offers numerous case studies.

Chiropractic Craniopathy is of great importance with respect to numerous health conditions, including concussions, head trauma, Attention Deficit Disorder (ADD) and Attention Deficit Hyperactivity Disorder (ADHD), Parkinson's, Multiple Sclerosis, dementia and all manner of brain disease and healing. Many books have been published on these subjects, several quite exhaustive; however, none of the current published books embrace the understanding of the importance of cranial function and the value of cranial therapies documented here.

This book provides the important missing piece to virtually all published information currently available on cranial therapies. It is my hope that **Brain Matters–The Missing Link** will greatly expand the understanding and application of Chiropractic Craniopathy and assist in *"Releasing the Hidden Healing Powers of Your Brain."*

Table of Contents

Acknowledgements xv

Preface xvii

Introduction 1

Part One 11

Chapter 1 - A History of Chiropractic Craniopathy 13

Chapter 2 - The Cranium 19

Chapter 3 - The Brain and Spine 25

Chapter 4 - Category II Subluxation Complex and
De Jarnette Cranial Syndrome 51

Chapter 5 - Cranial Distortion 89

Chapter 6 - Category II Self-Test 103

Chapter 7 - Cranial Adjustments and the Mind 107

Chapter 8 - Measuring Change 113

Part Two 129

Chapter 9 - Differentiating Symptoms for
Diagnostic Accuracy and Healing 131

Chapter 10 - Alternative Cranial Techniques 135

Chapter 11 - Occipital Fibers and Temporomandibular
Dysfunction (TMD) 151

Chapter 12 - Fibromyalgia 155

Chapter 13 - Detoxification 173

Chapter 14 - Other Alternative Therapies 183

Chapter 15 - Conclusion 189

Appendix A....................................... 197

Appendix B....................................... 213

Appendix C....................................... 215

Appendix D....................................... 219

Appendix E....................................... 221

Appendix F 223

Table of Illustrations 225

Table of Abbreviations............................ 227

Glossary... 229

Bibliography of Research Studies in Craniopathy 235

About the Author................................. 241

Index 243

Introduction

"Obstacles are those frightful things you see when you take your eyes off your goal."

– Henry Ford

Cindy was tired. It had been another very long day of another very long week. She was overworked and felt there was never enough time to commit to all the personal requirements needed for optimal health. She hadn't been sleeping well and her often relentless abdominal cramps were back. In addition to being tired, she was experiencing neck pain caused by a head trauma a few months earlier. Her pain and exhaustion were obvious.

I watched her intently as she gingerly eased herself onto the chiropractic table. As I listened to her litany of health issues, I intuitively knew what she needed. I suggested I perform a cranial adjustment. Cindy was familiar with the procedure, as I had described it to her previously. She readily agreed.

Forty-five minutes later, her body was visibly relaxed and appeared to melt into the table. I gave her a few minutes to sink into this new physical state. When she finally sat up, she was smiling. She closed her eyes again for a moment and let out a deep sigh. Opening her eyes, she asked, "How did you know what to do?"

"I don't know," I replied. "I just knew."

"My neck is so much better. I guess I do not need more x-rays after all. I think we know the cause of my problem. It is all in my head," she responded wryly.

I knew better than to make any of my usual wisecracks. She contin-ued, "My stomach cramps are gone, and I feel so much more relaxed and awake. I can tell already that I will sleep much better tonight."

"How can this be?" she asked. I replied that I could explain all the details, that not only would she be bored, her brain wasn't in any position to understand most of it right now.

She continued to quiz me, asking how her abdominal cramps and neck pain could be resolved by performing treatments on her head. Be-fore I could answer, she added that her lower back pain, which she hadn't mentioned, was also gone. I opened my mouth to answer, but she again interrupted, peppering me with several questions.

"Why is it that more doctors don't do this? Why isn't this more pop-ular? How come most physicians don't know about these kinds of treat-ments?"

She finally stopped to breathe. "Cindy," I said, "It would take a whole book just to begin to explain the basics."

With total conviction, she said, "Then you need to write it!"

So, I did.

Western Thinking versus Human Healing

Cindy's enthusiasm and insistence that this book be written came from her experience with the Integrated Sutural Protocol" (ISP), one facet of a host of procedures within the field of Chiropractic Craniopathy. Hers is, in fact, a common reaction to having the bones in the head manipulated ever so slightly. The movements might be small, but the resulting relief is a reaction I see repeatedly.

Yet most medical practitioners aren't aware that this and many other procedures exist. The reasons for this lack of awareness are numerous. It has to do with the way medical issues are studied and medicine is prac-ticed in our society. Modern Western medicine has a particular affinity for reductionist medical research. In other words, the research reduces the variables tested so that single pieces to the puzzle can be identified.

In this paradigm, thoroughly identifying every part of a system leads to understanding the whole. The ultimate goal is to identify a counteracting agent, usually pharmaceutically designed or other chemical substances, which can be applied to control the symptom or condition. It's believed that if scientists can understand the cause of the problem in its smallest and most specific detail, they can more accurately and definitively devise a program that will counteract or reverse the problem. However, everyone knows that the whole is greater than the sum of its parts, and while the reductionist theory is great for physics and math, it's in direct opposition to all the theories of human healing.

Vitalistic Healing

Throughout humankind's existence, individuals have sought to unravel the mysteries of healing. Investigators and philosophers through the ages have all reached a similar conclusion: the healing process is motivated by some mysterious energy. This healing energy has been called many names throughout history. The ancient acupuncturists called it "ki" or "chi" or "qi." Yogis called it "kundalini" and "prana." "Pneuma" and "Odic Force" are other old terms used. Samuel Hahnemann, MD called it the "Vital Force" and Dr. David D. Palmer dubbed it the "Innate Intelligence of the Body" or simply "Innate." More recently in Star Wars, it was referred to simply as "The Force." In chiropractic, it is called the "innate energy" or the "vital force."

Whatever name we use to describe the innate vital healing energy of the body, it remains a mysterious phenomenon that defies definition in mainstream scientific terms. There is, however, a small but growing body of traditional scientific evidence to support energetic healing properties. Some medical researchers, such as Bjorn E. W. Nordenstrom, MD in his book, *Biologically Closed Electric Circuits*, outlines a lifetime of research that supports this concept of energy movement in the body. Any serious student of energy medicine seeking tangible evidence should include this book in his or her studies.

This theory of vital force healing has come to be known as Vitalistic Healing. Vitalistic Healing doesn't attempt to exclude any scientific investigation or understanding, but instead aims to include all the endless, invisible and unknowable factors that reductionist science has yet to decipher or discover.

Reducing the healing process down to its smallest bits is fascinating, as any fan of reductionist theory will tell you. Healing is, however, far more complex than it may appear. Our bodies are meant to be self-healing. Except for certain notable diseases, many healing processes are self-sustaining. If a person cuts himself, the cut heals. If a person gets a cold or flu, she often finds that a few days are all it takes for the illness to resolve. If a person breaks a leg or experiences a trauma, the body eventually heals. The physician may assist in this process, as in setting a broken bone or stitching a wound, but the true healing forces are inherent or innate to the organism.

If for some reason the body is not healing as it normally would, there must be some interference with the natural healing mechanism. The healing vitality of the system is blocked from its innate expression; thus, the system cannot heal properly, causing symptoms or conditions to continue or worsen.

Blockages to the healing force are many and varied even from person to person. Just a few of the multitudes of possibilities may include diet and nutrition, vitamins and minerals, thoughts and belief systems, emotional conflicts and emotional traumas, as well as pinched nerves, structural misalignments, muscle problems, genetics, occupational stresses, and exercise or lack thereof. An almost inexhaustible list of blockages can be involved in compromising the healing process.

The true resolution of the disease comes when an intervention enables the inhibited, self-healing process to function properly again. The solution may be a vitamin, change in attitude or a spiritual experience. When the individual receives what he truly needs, the increased vitality will restore the innate mechanisms and processes, resulting in healing.

Often, the ultimate cure is unique to the individual. This uniqueness explains the diverse array of healing experiences. For example, if we questioned 100 people who have found relief from headaches, we would likely hear almost as many remedies. When the innate vital force of the body is enhanced by any means, the ability of the individual to self-heal is restored.

Vitalistic concepts open the door to multiple different healing possibilities. It doesn't reduce people down to a few cells; it allows for the whole to be treated, not just a few parts. Vitalism gives us great insight and direction in our attempts to assist ailing individuals.

A Case Study–Mrs. C

Mrs. C. had nagging neck, shoulder and low back pain for many, many years. She was still surprisingly active but suffered a great majority of the time with these complaints. She had been to many doctors all around the country with limited relief. She exercised daily and had good diet and nutrition. She was desperate but determined. She was also endlessly questioning and curious.

Never a day or treatment went by that she did not ask, "Why"? As best as I could, I tried to satisfy her curiosity but failed miserably. She probably does not realize it, but she became one of my best teachers. Her constant insistence on understanding compelled me to search for more and more answers. Mrs. C., I hope this book answers at least some of your questions.

My examination revealed that Mrs. C. was suffering from what we call a Category II subluxation complex. This will be discussed in much more detail in later chapters. A series of treatments designed to address the Category II structural distortions proved to be very useful for Mrs. C. Her pains began to diminish and progressively did so with subsequent treatments.

Our treatments were unfortunately very sporadic. This remarkable woman was heavily involved in a variety of charitable organizations and endeavors. These dedications often took her on trips away from home for extended periods of time.

I was happy that she was improving but it was entirely too slow. Because Mrs. C was not available for a consistent treatment program, we began thinking of strategies to accelerate her treatment.

Remembering the successful treatment developed by Dr. Major Bertrand De Jarnette, one of my mentors, I recognized that Mrs. C. needed a full sutural procedure for the De Jarnette Cranial Syndrome (DCS). The arrangements were made, and the treatment was provided.

Upon her next visit to the office, Mrs. C. had an interesting story to tell. The night of the treatment, she suddenly experienced a rapid onset of an asthma attack. Mrs. C. had experienced asthma symptoms for approximately 20 years. They were controlled with medications but would occasionally result in flare-ups.

This was one such asthma attack but different than usual. The specific characteristics of this attack were different than typical. The symptoms became surprisingly severe very quickly. She lived only a few city blocks from the hospital; however, by the time her husband drove her to the emergency room, she was almost back to normal. Very puzzling. I asked how she was doing since that night and she replied that her breathing was much better than in many years.

That night was the last asthma symptom Mrs. C. had. At our last contact she had been symptom-free and completely off all asthma medication for over five years since that first full sutural procedure.

I will be eternally grateful to Mrs. C for this experience. Until treating her I did not have a full appreciation for the potential of the DCS to impact human health. I also became much more aware of the innate healing capacity of the body when it is given the proper conditions. Witnessing the changes in Mrs. C as her Category II subluxation complex and DCS were corrected was insightful and inspirational.

But the question remains: how can correcting cranial subluxations result in the elimination of asthma symptoms? How is that possible and why is it that more physicians and other therapists do not know about these procedures? I hope the following pages provide some answers to those questions.

Mrs. C. continued treatments including sutural procedures, which all provided her with much relief from many of her chronic symptoms and conditions.

This case illustrates what science would call anecdotal information. It is a story about an experience that lacks a controlled research constraint. Antidotes are stories. This is, however, true a story. It is not a scientific investigation...well sort of.

Just because it is anecdotal and does not follow a structured scientific research design does not mean that it is untrue. This experience happened to a real live person. Many chiropractic physicians around the world have reported equally astounding results from their treatments using Chiropractic Craniopathy. Miraculous occurrences happen daily but are largely ignored by medical science.

In many ways this is for very good reasons. People's minds and imagination can be very misleading at times. Good science assures us honesty in our treatments. This should not, however, completely negate the real-world clinical experiences by people daily.

Unfortunately, in healthcare, many practitioners make a huge mistake when they have experiences, such as those witnessed by physicians like me and clients like Mrs. C. They tend to expect that the same treatment will be successful for all people with the same condition. There is a tendency to connect specific symptoms with specific treatments. It does not always work that way.

As you will come to understand throughout the pages of this book, it is not the procedure that effected the changes in Mrs. C's condition. Instead, I simply enabled her system to heal itself as it should. While you will come to understand how the sutural procedure can affect respiration, you will also appreciate that respiration affects the sutural mechanism. Most conditions experienced by people can be extremely complex. Therefore, the sutural procedure will not help all people or individuals who experience asthma. To make such a simple conclusion from this experience would be non-scientific, as well as completely erroneous.

However, one of the first tenants of scientific investigation is observation. While it would be unscientific to conclude that the sutural procedure helps all individuals with asthma, it would be equally unscientific to ignore the observation that the full sutural procedure for DCS indeed had a profound effect upon this individual with asthma.

As you continue to read this book, I hope you appreciate what you think you know and what you do not know about health. I hope we can also take the valuable lessons afforded us by individuals, such as Mrs. C., and her healing experiences by putting them into a perspective that is optimally useful for you in your life.

Until Mrs. C reported the resolution of her asthma symptoms, I would have considered this event to be impossible. There is no scientific evidence for this to occur. Yet it happened anyway. Very often we refuse to believe that health can be restored by non-conventional methods. We often even call it a 'spontaneous remission' when someone experiences relief when it is not supposed to happen by our scientific understanding.

These miraculous events are often discarded because we do not understand them. Instead, it would be a much more empowering strategy to look at the event and learn from it by exploring the healing systems that allowed it to happen. Miracles cease to be mysterious once the mechanism has been described. We need open minds and to conduct much more research.

Part One

"If the human brain were so simple
That we could understand it,
We would be so simple
That we couldn't."

– Emerson M. Pugh

Chapter 1
A History of Chiropractic Craniopathy

"In questions of science, the authority of a thousand is not worth the humble reasoning of a single individual."
– Galileo Galilei

Humans have been studying the human anatomy for centuries. From the ancient cultures to today in the twenty-first century, a desire to understand the human body has resulted in sometimes fantastical theorizing, as well as amazing discoveries.

It's believed Hippocrates, who lived in Greece in the 400s BC and considered the father of modern medicine, first theorized that the human cranium has an impact on our overall health. He wrote a treatise entitled *On Wounds in the Head*, which describes a variety of head wounds. Using only clinical observation, he accurately described the appearance of the skull and the effect fractures would have on it. This seminal work continues to inspire and educate physicians today.

A brief history of Chiropractic Craniopathy

Three men are considered modern-day pioneers in the field of Chiropractic Craniopathy:

- Dr. Nephi Cottam (1883-1966), a chiropractic physician, devised his own system of cranial therapies[1] and coined the term Chiropractic Craniopathy. Cottam reported his initial inspiration for Chiropractic Craniopathy in 1895. The first professional presentation was 27 January 1929, which was then reported in the newspaper on 20 February 1929. His first book was published in 1936. Later,

---

[1] http://www.biocranial.com/nonhealthcare/history.pdf

an example of his work is noted in a 1990 book work by his son, Calvin Cottam: *Cranial and Facial Adjusting: Sources, References, Index (Vol. 2)*. In it, the younger Cottam describes a procedure used by Dr. Cottam on a distraught, hysterical patient. With the patient in a seated position, he lifted her head ever so slightly up and away from her body to reposition it. This procedure, called a cephalad lift, provided immediate relief to the woman who had been suffering immeasurably for three days. Dr. Cottam's results were the basis for a new movement in chiropractic education beginning in the early 1930s and continuing today.

- Dr. William Garner Sutherland[2] (1873-1954), an osteopathic physician and contemporary of Dr. Cottam, taught the idea of a "Primary Respiratory Mechanism" in 1899. He subscribed to the idea, first proposed by Emmanuel Swedenborg, that all components within the body, including the cranium, expand and contract rhythmically. He also correctly noted that movement was possible between the cranial bones that could affect other areas or the entire person. He reached his conclusions after performing experiments to understand how the body functions. As is often the case in Western medicine, Dr. Sutherland's ideas were slow to take hold with other osteopaths until the early 1940s. His book, *Osteopathy in the Cranial Field*, published in 1951, has gone through several revisions and is still considered a valued resource on cranial techniques and concepts.

- Dr. Major Bertrand De Jarnette (1899-1992), was a chiropractic physician with a background in engineering and osteopathy. His original chosen occupation was the field of engineering. After being severely injured in an explosion in the factory where he was apprenticing, he was treated with osteopathic therapies to aid in his healing. Wishing to continue the osteopathic techniques used, he sought treatment after leaving the hospital but found it to be expen-

---

2 https://drgentile.com/WG%20Sutherland.htm

sive. Since students receive free treatments, De Jarnette enrolled in classes at the Dearborn College of Osteopathy. He found that chiropractic treatments were more effective for his condition and entered chiropractic college. His quest to understand human healing led to the Sacro Occipital Technic™ (SOT®) Methods of Chiropractic and Chiropractic Craniopathy, a system that integrates structure, function and cranial mechanisms into a whole-body approach.

Modern-day craniopathy however had roots beginning much earlier. Emanuel Swedenborg (1688-1772). From 1741 to 1744 he wrote 4 books totaling 2566 pages describing his brain research. In his books, *The Brain* volumes I and II and *The Cerebrum* volumes I and II he described cerebrospinal fluid, its importance in healing and the mechanisms of CSF flow. While Swedenborg lacked the luxuries of modern technology, he accurately described much of the mechanism upon which craniopathy is based.

More recently, Dr. John Upledger (1932-2012) developed cranial osteopathy into Cranial Sacral Therapy (CST). Upledger wrote several outstanding books on the subject and founded the Upledger Institute, still teaching his protocols worldwide.

The Sacro Occipital Technic™ (SOT®) Methods of Healing

Dr. Major Bertrand De Jarnette was truly a Renaissance man who wrote more than 130 books, thousands of pages of research papers and made numerous inventions. The intent of his life's work was to understand the human healing process. He came to understand that addressing symptoms was an inferior form of medicine and sought to understand the controlling mechanisms of the healing process. His research described the essential components of these systems. They are as follows:

- Category I – the cerebral spinal fluid flow mechanisms and functional neurology
- Category II – structural integrity and proprioceptive neurology
- Category III – connective tissue systems
- Trapezius Fiber System – fixations of the thoracic and lumbar spines
- Occipital Fiber System – neurological relationships with organ function
- Cranial System – addresses cranial subluxations
- Extremity System – addresses extremities subluxations and their relationships to neurological function
- Suboccipital Fiber System – central nervous system reflex syndromes
- Pain Control – addresses the neurological basis of pain syndromes
- Articular System – addresses alignment and mobility of various joints

Each of these systems have an extensive collection of diagnostic testing and specific therapeutic interventions to address chiropractic subluxations. These systems represent some of the fundamental healing mechanisms of the human body.

Treatment includes manipulative techniques, soft-tissue procedures, organ reflexes, neurological training, nutrition and a host of other interventions, as indicated by the diagnostics for each system and by individual needs and responses to treatments.

SOT and Craniopathic Training

Dr. De Jarnette realized that to understand and optimally execute all his discoveries and teachings, a person must first obtain his advanced degree in chiropractic medicine. Only then would he become eligible for the extensive training necessary to become certified in SOT.

To specialize in the SOT Methods of Chiropractic, the doctor must undergo a course of study specific to the Sacro Occipital Technic and SOT-Craniopathy. A minimum number of hours of post-doctorate study coupled with a minimum number of years of clinical experience are necessary to qualify for the standardized written and oral certification examinations, which are administered through Sacro Occipital Research Society, Inc. (SORSI) and its Sacro Occipital Teaching Organization (SO-TO-I) affiliates. Both must be passed. There are currently two levels of certification in SOT (without a cranial focus), *Certified Proficiency in the Philosophy, Art & Science of Sacro Occipital Technic and Advanced Proficiency in the Philosophy, Art & Science of Sacro Occipital Technic.* These certifications assure that the practitioner is skilled in SOT Methods.

To become eligible for the oral and written Craniopathic examinations, a chiropractic physician must complete at least five years of clinical SOT practice and the prescribed number of post-doctorate hours of study in the SOT Methods. The Craniopathic levels are *Certified Craniopath (CC) from the International Craniopathic Society (ICS), SORSI & SOTO-I, Diplomate International Craniopathic Society (DICS) and Fellow International Craniopathic Society (FICS).*

By the time a chiropractic physician reaches the "Fellow" certification, she has been practicing for at least 10 years, has attained all levels of proficiency and has presented a minimum of five SORSI or SOTO-I approved research papers and published at least one research paper in a SORSI/SOTO-I approved peer-reviewed journal. As of 2019, less than 200 individuals had received Craniopathic certification from ICS. This is truly an elite group of doctors. However, the advanced skills of any chiropractic physician certified in SOT at any level distinguish her from her colleagues.

Educational materials on Sacro Occipital Technic and SOT-Craniopathy are available through SORSI. However, only a certified Doctor
of Chiropractic as licensed by the local professional organizations are
authorized to utilize these techniques. Anyone can purchase, read and
study books on dentistry, surgery, pharmacology, etc. Knowledge alone
does not imply certification in the administration of these techniques
and procedures. Likewise, this book, its contents and any of its references
are for informational purposes only.

Armed with a basic understanding of SOT, the next chapter will
delve into human anatomy as a means of explaining the interrelatedness
of all bodily systems, starting with the head.

Chapter 2

The Cranium

*"When we try to pick out anything by itself, we find it
hitched to everything else in the Universe."*
~ John Muir

It's a common misconception that the human head is one solid mass of
bone whose sole function is to protect the delicate brain from an unfortunate incident. The truth is far more interesting. As noted in Chapter
1, the cranium or skull is actually composed of several pieces of bone
knitted together at joints, called sutures, giving the cranium flexibility.

Because of its makeup, the cranium is in constant motion. With our
every breath and every movement, it is moving. Any action made with
the body triggers motion responses in the cranium. While these motions
are quite small, they are vitally important for optimal neurological functioning and, in turn, the health of the entire body, mind and spirit.

There are 22 bones in the human cranium. Of these, the seven cranial bones of major importance to this discussion are parietal bones (2),
temporal bones (2) and one each of the occiput, sphenoid and frontal
bones. When you breathe in, each bone moves in one direction. Breathing out induces motion in the opposite direction. While the movement
is in the range of only a few ten thousandths of an inch, it is essential to
our health and well-being.

Additionally, different cranial bone movements occur due to mechanical actions of the spine and pelvis. When you walk, your cranium
exhibits certain reciprocal motions with the hips. Turning of the head
and other movements of the spine induce different motions in the head.
With each step that you take, every turn of your head or bend of your

body, there are structural forces that transmit stresses and strains into the cranium that cause motion. If cranial motion is lost for any reason, negative consequences will most certainly occur. Sometimes the effects can be devastating.

Dr. De Jarnette was the first to describe the two different cranial motions. The first relates to respiration, movement associated with the breath. The second is structural, associated with mechanical motions of the whole body. Disturbances in each must be diagnosed and treated differently. Dr. De Jarnette is also the only investigator to identify the De Jarnette Cranial Syndrome (DCS) and provide the effective treatment protocol for the structural subluxations through the full Integrated Sutural Protocols (ISP).

In addition, talking and chewing impact upon the cranial bones. Conversely, the cranial bones also affect the jaw, sometimes producing temporomandibular joint dysfunction (TMD). There are reciprocal relationships like this throughout the body and they are referred to as "reciprocal mechanisms." Reciprocal mechanisms are like seesaws. Each end is inseparably related to the other. Whenever something happens to one end (or side) of the mechanism, an equal and opposite effect occurs on the other end. While there are numerous reciprocal relationships occurring in the human body, for the purposes of our discussion, the most important ones are:
- Occiput and sacrum (base of skull and tailbone)
- Ilium and temporal bone on the same side (hip bone and side bone of the head)
- Right and left temporal bones
- Right and left hip bones (ilia)
- Category II pelvic subluxation complex and DCS

According to the law of reciprocal relationships:

- Any subluxation (misalignment or aberration of motion) of the occiput bone will produce an equal and opposite disturbance in the sacrum.

- All subluxations of the sacrum will produce an equal and opposite stress into the occiput.

- All subluxations of the right hip affect the right temporal bone (same on left).

- All subluxations of the right temporal bone will cause an equal and opposite stress into the left temporal bone (opposite is also true).

The above structures are all interrelated and a disturbance in one part affects all the others. This is a basic and simple description of structural reciprocity. Like dominoes, one piece of the chain triggers a collection of effects. Once any subluxation complex is established, there may be several complications. Successful treatment of the Category II subluxation complex may therefore require varied and different treatment procedures, sometimes seemingly unrelated. A properly certified SOT chiropractic physician may find it necessary to treat additional parts of your body to obtain the desired healing response.

Technically speaking, the reciprocal relationships described above are true most of the time. While normal body motions produce equal and opposite effects, in some cases of serious conditions or trauma, parts of these relationships can become fixated or even displaced to an extent that prevents normal reciprocal motions. Such situations can be the source of many unresolved problems for the person. All too often, doctors only search the symptoms presented and fail to uncover and treat the underlying cause of the problem.

Causes of Cranial Subluxations

Disturbances in the minute motion and/or misalignments of cranial bones (cranial subluxations) can be due to any number of causes. Any prolonged or severe stress, whether mental, emotional or physical can contribute to or cause cranial subluxations. The most obvious is traumatic injury. Interestingly, the injury does not need to be directly to the head to affect the cranium. Trauma can be to the neck, anywhere in the spine or the hips or low back.

Cranial subluxations are dysfunctions of the cranial bones and can manifest in many forms. In some cases, cranial bones may not be moving properly, which in turn inhibits the function of the Cranial Sacral Respiratory Mechanism (CSRM). Another possibility is fixation of the entire cranial sutural system known as the De Jarnette Cranial Syndrome (DCS), which is commonly associated with the Category II subluxation complex.

The effects of cranial subluxations on the patient can range from mild to devastating. Could this be a silent killer among us? While there have been no mainstream medical tests found to date that identify or diagnose these types of cranial bone dysfunctions, in the chiropractic profession we have found the negative impact of cranial subluxations to be undeniable. This includes DCS, as well as hundreds of other possible cranial subluxations.

Most traditional physicians have never even heard of cranial subluxations, DCS or the Category II subluxation complex, and may discount their existence, even if they have. Chiropractic physicians worldwide have successfully treated many "incurable conditions" using the techniques of Chiropractic Craniopathy.

Cranial subluxations often afflict individuals suffering from closed head injuries and other stresses and traumas. These people frequently suffer unexplained and seemingly untreatable symptoms. Often, when all traditional treatments fail or the medical tests appear to be normal, they are told that they have a psychiatric illness. The unfortunate patient, who is likely in severe physical, mental and/or emotional pain, begins to believe that he is making it up in his head.

Sometimes symptoms and conditions stemming from cranial subluxations in general and DCS specifically will even go unnoticed. They can be insidious and may include fatigue, sleep problems, digestive disturbances, mood changes, etc. These symptoms can subtly evolve over time, making it impossible to identify the initial injury. A direct connection with a stress or trauma is not always obvious or readily apparent. Worse still, any connection between the injury and stress causing the cranial subluxation and the developing symptoms are commonly dismissed by the experts as unrelated.

I have personally observed this exact situation with many young patients. I had an opportunity to work with several young children suffering from epileptic seizures. Each mother reported that her child began to suffer from seizures after a blow to the head from a fall. Pediatricians declared this to be impossible. Instead, the explanation was that the child had a seizure, which caused her to fall and sustain a head injury. The possibility the seizures were caused by a cranial subluxation from a head injury was immediately discounted, and therefore, never diagnosed. Since traditional medicine does not believe in cranial bone subluxations, the true cause of trauma-induced cranial misalignment can't be diagnosed by traditional medical tests.

The fact remains that many of these children have been successfully treated with proper cranial diagnosis and correction. Chiropractic Craniopaths have reported good results with seizure cessation and other conditions. By addressing the cranial subluxations, I have several patients who are now seizure free. When one understands the mechanics of the Craniosacral Respiratory Mechanism (CSRM), it becomes apparent that the function of the brain can indeed be severely compromised by cranial subluxations and DCS.

To complicate matters even further, head issues or cranial subluxations can arise from other problems in the body, not just from a hit on the head. Trauma or injury in areas such as the neck, back or hips can produce cranial changes, which can result in a variety of debilitating symptoms or conditions. Furthermore, trauma is not the only avenue to cranial dysfunction. Stress affecting organs and muscles can also bring about cranial dysfunction. These stresses can stem from diet, toxicity, mental and emotional issues, etc.

The cranium is only the beginning of the fascinated interconnectedness of the body. Next, we'll explore the brain and nervous system, as well as other systems that make life, as we know it, possible.

Chapter 3

The Brain and Spine

"The mind, once stretched by a new idea, never returns to its original dimensions."
> – Ralph Waldo Emerson

The brain is safely housed in the cranial bowl surrounded by material crucial to the brain's survival. In the image below, the various layers are identified. Each serves a specific purpose. The topmost layer is the cranium, which is the bony shell discussed in Chapter 2. The next layers are called the cranial meninges, which are formed by the outermost layer called dura mater, the collagen-filled layer called arachnoid mater (so named because the collagen looks like spider webs) and the innermost and softest layer called the pia mater. There is also a small channel called the subarachnoid space between the arachnoid mater and pia mater that houses the cerebrospinal fluid, as well as cerebral arteries and veins. The term "mater" means "mother" in Latin. In this context, you can consider these three layers as protective "mothers" to the brain.

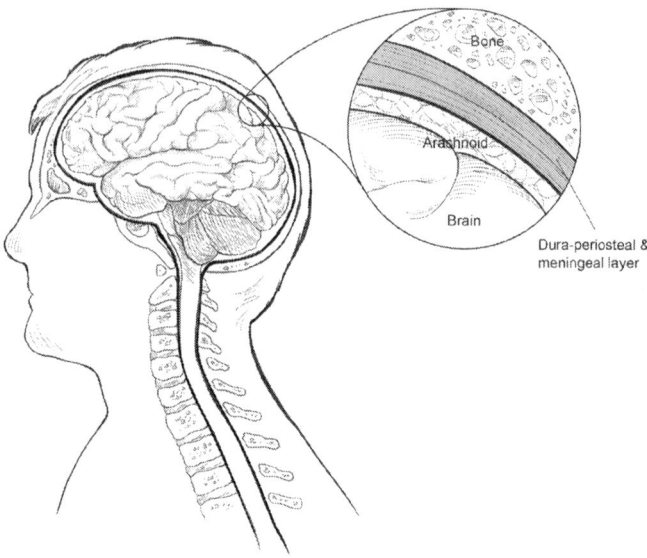

Figure 1: *The Dura Mater engulfs the brain somewhat like a balloon ending in a tube that travels down the spine and anchors in the sacrum of the pelvis. The dura is flexible but not elastic. Any stresses placed into the dura will produce a pulling force up and down the spine into the cranium, pelvis and attachments throughout the entire spinal column. The dura and all these bones are in constant motion producing a pump for cerebral spinal fluid, providing nutrition for the brain and lymph to remove waste products. Distortions or restrictions in any of the structures can impede these essential processes.*

The layer SOT-trained chiropractic physicians are interested in is the dura mater. The dura is a dense, tough, fibrous membrane. It is the only layer that has its own blood supply. It also has nerves making it the only entity in the cranial cavity sensitive to pain. The dura is responsible for pumping cerebrospinal fluid (CSF), which is vital for brain function. Both CSF and the dura mater will be discussed in more detail later in this chapter.

The Brain

The brain is only one part of the most complex and sophisticated machine on the planet — the human body. At the start of life, the body builds itself from two tiny cells to about 50 trillion cells in the average adult. The directions, blueprints and architectural plans for this growth are located in the DNA code of those first two cells. The resulting body is designed to be self-building, self-repairing and self-regulating. All these diverse functions are guided through nerve impulses from the brain.

The human brain represents about two percent of total body weight; however, it uses close to 20 percent of the oxygen and 15 to 25 percent of the blood supply. It works hard generating nearly 25 watts of energy through neurological signals. In fact, every function, motion and organ in the body is under the direct influence or control of the nervous system, of which the brain is the mastermind.

The brain has approximately 85 billion nerve cells. Each nerve cell connects from 1,000 to 10,000 other cells producing a vast and complex neurological network. Brain cells communicate with each other in determining what signals to transmit down the spine to the rest of the body. Each of the 85 billion cells is firing nerve signals at a minimum of 10 per second. Nerve signals can travel nearly 250 mph (112 meters per second) to coordinate body functions quickly and efficiently.

The nerve signals directing all the functions of the body are transmitted from the brain through 62 spinal nerves neatly packaged in 31 pairs. Additionally, there are 12 pairs (24 in total) of nerves that come out of holes (foramina) in the head called cranial nerves. These 86 nerves direct brain communication to every cell of the body. While the brain sends out information, it's also receiving information, since another function of the nervous system is reporting to the brain about what is happening throughout the body. The nervous system does this back-and-forth dance almost from the moment of conception until death.

The brain, through the nerves, also controls all muscle function. The tone and activity of the approximately 700 muscles of the body are controlled by these nerves at the rate of 20 to 200+ signals per second! All is well if connections are maintained. When a muscle loses its nerve connection, as when a nerve is cut, the muscle ceases to function. Without a nerve signaling it to move, the muscle won't move. It immediately goes into a state of flaccid paralysis, eventually withering from lack of use. The brain and its central nervous system are truly command central.

Occipital Fibers

Occipital fibers are tiny filaments located inside the cranium on the back of the head. Dr. De Jarnette was the first to discover these fibers. They have reflexes related to vertebrae in the spine and to the function of the organ associated with that specific vertebra. It took Dr. De Jarnette several decades to untangle all the pieces of the occipital fiber system including its function and how to treat it. We now know that occipital fibers enter through the base of the skull and attach to the dura that covers the brain. Tension on these fibers could easily produce stress in the dura, resulting in pain (such as headaches) or cranial dysfunction.

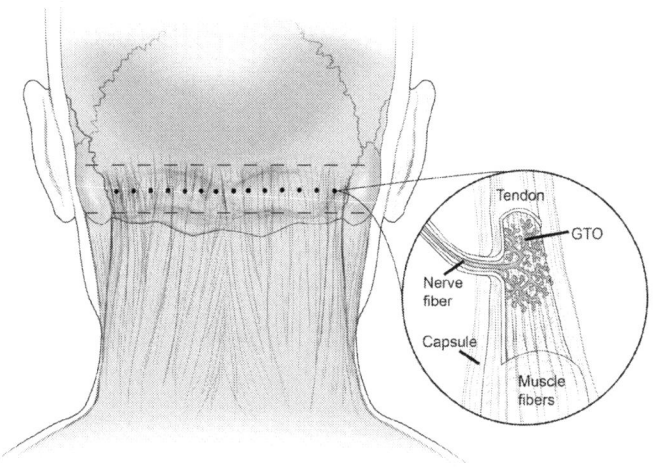

Figure 2: *Dr. Major Bertrand De Jarnette reported tiny fibers in the back of the skull that have a neurological relationship to a variety of subluxations and organ dysfunctions throughout the body. Along with research by Arthur Guyton MD and others, De Jarnette mapped the structure and function of these relationships. A quarter of a century later, medical anatomists finally discovered these fibers, originally reported by Dr. De Jarnette. The findings were first reported in an article in the 1998 Medical and Health Annual by Encyclopedia Britannica, Inc., titled "The Anatomist's New Tools."*

These little fibers react to nerve impulses generated by a stressed organ in the body. The organ function can be disturbed by nerve blockage from the spine, mental or emotional stress, nutritional deficiencies and imbalances and/or diseases and medical conditions.

When an organ is stressed, whether or not we feel any symptoms, the body reacts by sending signals to the brain. Under the proper circumstances, these signals will trigger a reaction in the occipital fiber. This fiber may become swollen or tender, or it can also go undetected for years or decades. It can, however, be the cause of headaches or other alterations in cranial function. It can impede normal cranial bone motion, which is essential for brain and nervous system function. It may also produce cranial distortions that result in cranial nerve dysfunction.

If not detected, the fibers can remain triggered for years or decades causing recurring headaches or other alterations in cranial function. They can impede normal cranial bone motion, which is essential for brain and nervous system function. They may also produce cranial distortions that can result in cranial nerve dysfunction.

Part of the possible anatomical basis for this mechanism was not discovered until 1998. The story of this research is quite fascinating, as follows:

Gary D. Hack DDS, Gwendolyn Dunn DDS and Mi Young Toh MS, MA took two cadavers and examined them with MRI pictures. MRIs make pictures that are slices of the anatomy. Each body was sliced in three different directions. Many thousands of slices were taken and then all the information was fed into a computer system to produce three-dimensional models of the bodies.

Two new findings were uncovered. The information was reported in the Encyclopaedia Britannica 1998 medical and health annual. The title of the article was The Anatomists New Tools.

The first surprise was a muscle in the jaw that had never been found before. This newly discovered structure was named the sphenomandibularis muscle. Its story is very revealing in its illustration of fundamental human nature. Of the many hundreds and hundreds of thousands of human dissections that have been undertaken over hundreds of years, no one had ever discovered this muscle. How can that possibly be?

As it turns out, every anatomist for all of history has always followed the standard dissection procedures. This is the set of directions for dissection; everyone does it exactly the same, every time. In fact, the way this particular procedure is performed destroys the sphenomandibularis muscle; therefore, it had never been found before. It is automatically destroyed by every standard dissection.

What is the lesson in this? If you are always looking for the same things you may not find something new, even though it has been there forever. "If you always do what you have always done you will always get what you have always gotten."

The other structures that were found in this groundbreaking study included little fibers attaching from inside the skull to the muscle in the back of the head. These tiny fiber connections are in the exact location of those that De Jarnette described. He called it the occipital fiber system in man. Is it possible that these anatomists finally found the structures that De Jarnette described 50 years earlier? Not only is this entirely possible, but it would account for some of the symptoms that are often present when there is an occipital fiber problem.

The fibers "discovered" in the recent MRI study attach to the back of the neck muscles and then to the occiput bone of the skull. Furthermore, they enter through the base of the skull and are attached to the Dura that covers the brain. Tension on these fibers could easily produce stress into the Dura and resulting pain (such as headaches) or cranial dysfunction.

These findings explain why a Sacral Occipital Technic (SOT®) certified chiropractic physician performs occipital fiber diagnosis. This analysis assists the doctor in determining the appropriate treatments to help your body resolve a complaint or symptom. Your doctor may also, with the insights afforded by the occipital fiber diagnosis, perform specific organ reflexes and/or suggest specific nutrition and supplements to address headaches, jaw problems or other issues in the neck, head and elsewhere in the body.

The human machine is glorious and complex. Symptoms, conditions and complaints may require treatment in totally different parts of the body for the best possible results. See Appendix F for a case study involving TMJ function and the occipital fiber relationship to cranial function.

The occipital fiber system is unique to the SOT diagnosis and healing. It can be any essential tool in the diagnosis and treatment of some head conditions. Almost any symptom anywhere in the body can be caused from inside the head. But not all had symptoms are caused from the head.

It can be very difficult to accurately determine the cause of the many symptoms and conditions. Your healthcare practitioner of any discipline, be it medical, chiropractic, massage, acupuncture, psychology, etc. has a truly daunting task.

Therefore, if you are not achieving the results you desire, and your healthcare practitioner does not have a plausible plan to uncover the mysteries of your condition, it may be time to try something different. Sometimes something very different is what the doctor ordered.

The Cerebrospinal Fluid (CSF)

For the brain and its 85 (or more) billion nerve cells to function properly, the surrounding environment in the cranial cavity is critical. CSF is the necessary ingredient to maintaining a healthy brain and nervous system. CSF has been called many names: "the water of life," "the nectar of life," "the divine fluid," "tears of the Sky God" and "the tears of Christ." CSF is produced in the brain at about 500 ml (roughly one-half quart) per day. It carries the proper nutrition and maintains the precise environment required for optimal brain function. The entire brain is refreshed with CSF three to four times daily.

CSF is made deep inside the brain in the choroid plexuses located in the lateral, third and fourth ventricles. Although CSF is created from blood plasma, it is differentiated by its lack of protein cells and modified electrolytes. It brings nutrition to the brain and nervous system, buffers the brain from outside influences and provides resistance to harmful substances. It also serves a vital function maintaining stable cerebral blood flow. CSF is found in the subarachnoid space and the ventricular system inside and around the brain, as well as in the central canal that houses the spinal cord.

CSF is manufactured and moves about its assigned space under pressure. During its manufacture, pressure builds in the choroid plexus as each fills with CSF. Once critical pressure is reached, tiny valves open and cerebral spinal fluid is pushed into the ventricles. After the pressure is equalized, the valves close and the process begins anew. The pushing out and pressure release of the CSF is thought to be the pulsations that Dr. Sutherland described in his theory of Primary Respiratory Mechanism.

The distribution and flow of cerebral spinal fluid is under the direct control of the Craniosacral Respiratory Mechanism (CSRM), also known as the craniosacral pump. In other words, the motion of the cranial bones pumps CSF through and out of the brain. This mechanism undergoes a rhythmical pumping action on the average of six to eight times per minute and assists CSF flow out of the brain and through the spine.

Function of the brain and nervous system is dependent upon correct cerebrospinal fluid pressures and flow. CSF distribution depends on the CSRM. The CSF mechanisms are also protective and surprisingly tolerant of stresses and traumas. However, if great enough, the CSF pump can be impaired by structural imbalance, such as the Category II subluxation complex and the DCS. These can be enormously disruptive to the function of the brain, nervous system and the body at large.

While our bodies are far more sophisticated than cars, the mechanics involved allow for an adequate analogy. For your car to run properly, there are certain mechanisms that can't be out of alignment or out of shape by more than a 10,000th or sometimes 100,000th of an inch. In other words, while the car can withstand bangs, bumps, and weather extremes, if a critical part is the least little bit misshapen or misaligned, it can have disastrous effects upon the functioning of the whole machine.

The same is true for the human body. We are rugged and capable of enduring many mental, emotional and physical stresses and insults yet remain self-healing. However, a tiny misalignment in cranial structures can result in intense suffering elsewhere in the body.

The Dura

The dura is considered one of the most important parts of the CSRM. Without it, CSF wouldn't flow. The dura is a leather-like, fibrous yet pliable substance, sometimes described as being like a stainless-steel mesh. This is an apt description because the dura, like stainless steel, can't be stretched or pulled out of shape. In other words, if you pull on the dura, it doesn't stretch or give. If you tug on the dura at the top of the head, that tug will reverberate through the CSRM system all the way to the sacrum unless there is a blockage somewhere along the way. This strong yet semi-rigid construction allows for the non-stop pumping of CSF.

The dura has attachments to the bones of the skull, upper cervical spine (C-1, C-2 and C-3) and the sacrum (the triangular shaped bone at the base of the spine, between the hips) as well as throughout the spine via thin hair-like filaments called "dendritic" attachments. These run from the dura to the bone surface on the inside of the spinal canal. While the bones of the spine have attachments of muscles that allow us to sit and stand upright and move around, they also have other jobs. The spine and each vertebra have a canal or hole that connect at the base of the skull all the way down to the tailbone. This is the spinal canal.

The spinal canal provides a safe place for the spinal cord to live. The spinal cord houses the collection of nerves that direct function throughout the body. Because of the spinal column's importance to bodily function, the bones of the spine protect it.

The spine has several functions beyond a safe home for the nerves of the spinal cord. It gives anchor points for the muscles of the spine that allow us to move and incorporates the joints that are essential for that motion. There is an intimate relationship between all the nerves of the entire spine (spinal cord) and the spinal column. In addition, an intimate connection exists between the spinal column, cranium and the sacrum through the dura. Any mechanical stressing of this structure can transmit mechanical stresses throughout the entire structure. A simplistic illustration of this concept is that of a pulley system, as shown below.

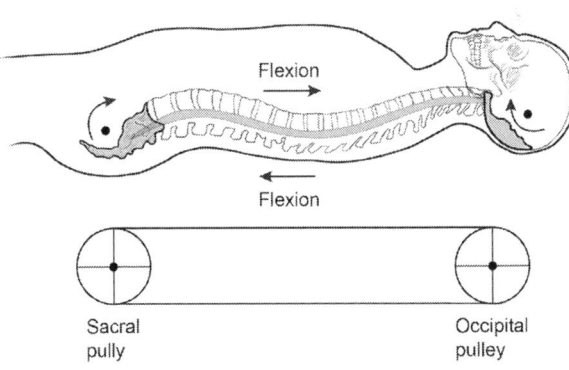

Figure 3: *The relationship between the occiput and sacrum is illustrated as a pulley system. The two ends are connected by dura and respond to each other in a synchronized fashion when functioning normally.*

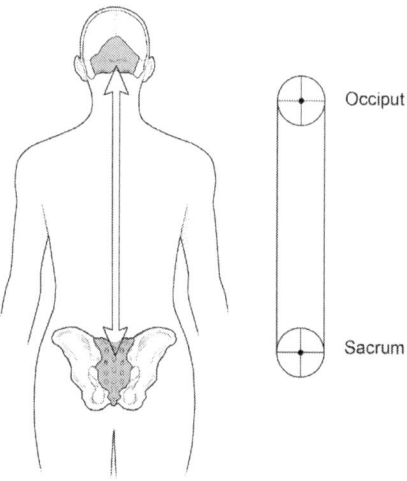

Figure 4: *This drawing depicts an additional dimension to this motion.*

The dura system is not a simple linear pulley system, however. It also transmits torqueing or twisting type distortions as shown in the illustration.

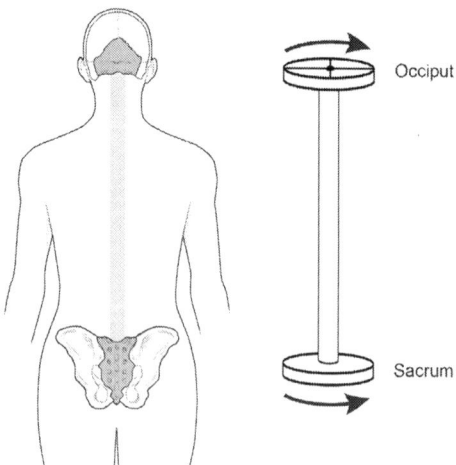

Figure 5: *The third vector of motion is further illustrated here. This torsional or twisting motion is frequently not described in much of the literature but plays an important part in the De Jarnette Cranial Syndrome (DCS).*

In addition, the dura forms sleeve-like attachments at the nerve roots of the vertebra. These dural sleeves protect the nerves as they exit the central nervous system and travel into the peripheral nervous system, which distributes nerve flow and the innate healing vitality through the entire body.

CSF Flow and the Dura

In his lifetime of research, Dr. De Jarnette concluded that the most important factor in healing is the CSF system. Simply, CSF flow is of primary importance to the optimal function of the central nervous system. It is of the essence that the CSRM function optimally to maintain health and healing. His conclusion as to the importance of CSF is the foundational belief on which his SOT is based.

CSF distribution is dependent upon the CSRM, which is comprised of the cranium, spinal column, sacrum and, most importantly, the dura and all its attachments. Any stress or strain, distortion or dysfunction anywhere in the entire CSRM affects the dura.

As noted above, the dura is attached in the upper cervical spine at C-1, C-2 and C-3. C-1, known as the Atlas, is the vertebrae on which the head sits. C-2, the Axis, sits below the Atlas and has a bony protrusion that holds the Atlas in place while allowing it to rotate. Together, these vertebrae create the C-1-C-2 cervical complex.

Because the C-1-C-2 cervical complex has the greatest amount of motion in the entire system, the attitude or position of these segments is affected by a disturbance elsewhere in the system. Therefore, it's quite common to find these two vertebral segments in a state of misalignment because they compensate and adapt to true subluxations elsewhere in the body. This finding led a handful of chiropractic researchers to conclude that, if the C-1-C-2 cervical complex is misaligned, it is causing problems in other parts of the system.

There are times when these vertebral segments are truly part of the problem. The SOT system identifies when the Atlas or Axis are fixated or subluxated and require direct intervention. However, a majority of the time, the efforts of SOT practitioners are focused on identifying and correcting the causes of dural system dysfunction that produced the upper cervical disturbance.

One of the most prominent dysfunctions described in SOT is the Category II distortion complex. This disturbance is often found to have its roots in a twisted pelvis. Through the dura, this twist produces a similar disturbance in the cranial mechanisms, creating a reciprocal distortion of the cranial structures and their dural attachments. In other words, a misaligned pelvis creates a similar misalignment in the head through the dural system.

With the cranial structures misaligned, the flow of CSF in the cranium is impeded. The result can be altered pressures in the various cranial compartments, as well as an increase in overall cranial pressure. This impeded flow and increased pressure encourage the associated central nervous system disturbances. If left unchecked, the increased pressure is believed to force CSF to breach the blood-brain barrier and leak into brain tissues. Current research suggests that when this occurs, autoimmune reactions are triggered, resulting in inflammation in the brain.

The CSF flow mechanisms are of ultimate importance in the function of the human nervous system. Disturbances and distortions anywhere in the entire structure can negatively affect CSF flow, leading to a multitude of diseases and conditions.

Misalignment Impact

Various distortions or subluxations can stress the dura and pull on the bones to which it's attached. These mechanical displacements can have devastating effects on the delicate nerves, as the neurological system is extremely sensitive to pressure and CSF flow. Distortions can impair neurological function throughout the entire body until properly corrected.

In their 1906 book, *The Science of Chiropractic: Its Principles and Adjustments*, Drs. DD and BJ Palmer expressed distortions in this way:

> *The brain sends its messages through the spinal cord to all parts of the body. The spinal marrow passes down through the spinal canal, and contains nerves, which control the nervous system and tactile impressions. The nerves branch out from the spinal cord in all directions, absolutely controlling every part of the anatomy. So potent is this control that all action, whether normal or abnormal, is absolutely dependent upon the condition of the nerve radiating from the spine. A wrench of the vertebral column invariably leads to some disturbance of that portion to which the nerves proceed and end. (p. 34)*

Our structural integrity, balance and alignment are all maintained through muscle integrity. Imbalance and misalignments can put pressure on the nerves in a way that prevents proper communication to the muscles, which creates a communications dilemma. If the structure is out of balance due to subluxations, the nerves can't do their jobs properly. Distorted messages are sent to the affected muscles. The result is impaired body alignment. Neurological function and structural balance are intimately interrelated. Each affects the other.

Therefore, the two major aspects involved in health are structure and function. When either of these becomes imbalanced, both tend to follow patterns of distortion that affect the whole body. In other words, a misaligned foot bone may cause a minute distortion resulting in a subluxation pattern all the way up to the cranium. These stress patterns, called subluxation patterns or distortion patterns, can produce symptoms at the site of the imbalance, but not always. Often symptoms develop in a different part of the body, far from the original source of the imbalance. Many of these structural stress patterns have been mapped out over decades of investigation. Neurological function is far harder to predict then structural imbalance.

The smallest misalignment can have a huge impact. To illustrate, imagine a high-rise building. Its construction must be exact for it to stand tall and straight. Yet, if one corner of the building is constructed a fraction of an inch lower, that fraction is multiplied through every floor of the building. Instead of it standing straight and tall, the building would have a decided lean on one corner thanks to that fractional mistake. Our bodies respond in the same way when a misalignment is present.

Dr. Hugh B. Logan, founder of Logan College of Chiropractic (now Logan University) and a pioneer in body biomechanics, discovered that structural imbalances double in their effects at critical points as we move up the human structural chain. In other words, the 16th of an inch discrepancy in leg length becomes a quarter of an inch discrepancy in the pelvis at the sacrum (tailbone). Above that, the next distortion will be a half an inch, etc. — just like a building!

This imbalance puts greater stress upon the lumbar spine disks, muscles and so on. It is no wonder that according to the concepts of the Logan Basic System of biomechanics, the disks of the bottom vertebra (the 5th lumbar) can often be squeezed out to one side causing disk herniation or even, as the distortion continues, a rupture.

Luckily, the brain is sensitive to imbalances. It will tell muscles (through the nerves) to compensate to minimize or limit some of these forces as they make their way up the body. In theory, this is great. However, the compensation for structural imbalances can lead to additional issues or problems.

The body is a complex system with multiple aspects of adaptation and compensation, each subject to a unique set of rules and regulations. Often, when evaluating an individual, what we see is a combination of several major factors contributing to the current condition.

The subluxations and imbalances described in this book provide insight into the problems that manifest in Dr. De Jarnette's Category II subluxation complex and DCS. The first case study exemplifies these imbalances.

Case Study – Anthony

Anthony was tough as nails and sharp as a tack. He'd spent his career in the Army as a paratrooper. He excelled at everything he attempted. He was always the leader of the pack, first in every race and always at the top of his class, until the unthinkable happened. While performing at an air show, one of his fellow paratroopers passed too close below and "stole his air." Anthony's parachute collapsed, and he went into a free fall to the ground. Miraculously, he survived. He sustained multiple fractures and his healing was a long and difficult process.

Attitude was paramount with Anthony. He never complained and always exhibited a positive outlook. He never felt sorry for himself. Instead, he saw his injuries as an opportunity to move in a new direction. He was inspired to go to Chiropractic College and enrolled at Logan University. The problem was that while Anthony was still tough as nails inside, the attack had taken a serious toll on his body and memory. He religiously continued his dietary and exercise regimens, despite the ongoing pain and discomfort, but his razor-sharp memory was severely compromised.

After completing an examination on him, it was clear he was suffering from a Category II subluxation complex. The trauma had left his sacroiliac joint, and many others, hypermobile (too loose). The stress caused by hypermobility in his pelvis traveled through the dura mater all the way to the cranium. His head bones had locked down so tightly that normal cranial motion was greatly diminished and CSF flow severely compromised. His brain wasn't getting all the required resources to maintain optimal functioning. The trauma had produced a severe case of DCS.

Anthony studied and worked out harder than everyone else did. Physically, he could make the grade even though there was more pain than he'd had in the past, but he found himself unable to remember information as he once did. So, he studied harder. To compensate for the additional time he had to spend studying, he worked out even harder to maintain his physical condition.

Despite extra studying, he would often have to take examinations over and even repeat some classes. Never discouraged and never complaining when faced with a setback, he would simply work harder to compensate for the shortcomings. Anyone else would have given up much earlier in the educational process. He had an unshakable dream. He was going to earn his Doctorate degree in Chiropractic and go to Australia to practice.

Before he could make his dream happen, he had to pass the four-part national board examinations and be licensed in the U.S. Anthony failed many of these examinations several times. He endured the embarrassment and financial strain (they are expensive) and worked even harder, eventually completing each of them successfully. But his testing days were not over. He still had to pass the "boards" in Australia, known for being difficult for foreigners because the education system was different.

At my suggestion, he agreed to a full sutural treatment. Anthony had received many chiropractic adjustments and other treatments throughout his course of studies, but none perform the same function as ISP. Fortunately, this initial procedure produced a significant pain reduction and increased his physical function. He felt better than he had since his parachute accident. It looked like we were on the right track.

On faith, he had made the trip to Australia to attend interviews and arrange a seat at the next Australian national board examinations. This was an enormous commitment and expenditure. It was also a risky venture mentally, emotionally and financially.

Two weeks before Anthony was to go to Australia to sit for his licensing examinations, we met at a chiropractic conference. I was able to give him another full sutural treatment. This time, he responded well. It seemed as if his cranium was more responsive than during the first treatment. He had begun the healing process.

When I saw him the next day, I was taken aback at his appearance. His face had visually changed. He didn't look the same as he did the day before. Fortuitously, I had taken a pre- and post-treatment photograph of him, as I had been exploring whether there were visible changes in a person's face before and after the full cranial sutural procedure. The difference was astonishing.

He reported waking with a severe headache that had lasted the entire day. As with any other adversity, he simply took it in stride and then chose to view it as a positive sign of progress. Indeed, it was.

When we met the following day, he described feeling as if his brain had been turned back on. His memory was back. He reported that he felt sharper and clearer mentally than he had since the parachute accident. He also felt like his old energy was back. Everything with his body and his mind felt easier, more like it used to be several years earlier.

But the true test was still waiting. Would he be able to muster the recall necessary to pass the Australian Board examinations and realize his dream? After all, many of the native physicians in Australia do not pass these examinations the first time, even though they are a product of the Australian educational system.

In the following weeks, Anthony not only successfully passed all the Australian chiropractic board examinations; he achieved the second highest grade of all those taking it at that time. He is now living his dream as a practicing chiropractic physician in Australia.

Anthony still experiences some fallout from his injuries, but to date (ten years and counting) he has maintained most of his positive progress after the full cranial sutural procedures. Practicing in a rather remote area in Australia, he does not have access to continued Chiropractic Cranial treatments. However, he is still committed to exercising, eating a healthy diet and maintaining a positive attitude to support his rediscovered structural integrity and cranial sutural functions.

Anthony's cognitive functions were devastated by his injuries. Those effects persisted long after the physical cuts, bruises and numerous fractures had healed. He also suffered a great deal of pain that didn't appear to have a physical cause. His body's response to the full cranial procedure felt to him nothing short of miraculous.

I would not be surprised if the persistent effects experienced in people who have experienced a traumatic brain injury are at least in part due to DCS. Many factors are undoubtedly involved; however, the cranial sutural system is probably the most overlooked, due to the lack of awareness and understanding in the medical community at large, as well as a great majority of chiropractic providers.

A head injury might seem like a "no-brainer" for the full sutural procedure. It's less obvious this is needed when the complaint is excruciating low back pain, as in the case of Michael.

Case Study - Michael

I met Michael at our local dog park. Initially, I knew all of Michael's dog's names but not his. After running into each other enough times, we started talking.

Michael was tall, blonde and well-built, as well as intelligent, self-assured and friendly. I learned that he had been working as a schoolteacher until a car accident some months earlier changed his life. An inattentive driver hit him from the side causing a lateral whiplash. To combat the immediate pain he felt, he went to physical therapy and saw a physician until his insurance benefits ran out. Then, he was told that there was nothing else that could be done for him and he was discharged from treatment.

The debilitating low back pain continued. Anyone who has suffered in pain can understand how it might affect the emotions and be exhausting to manage. Michael began to suffer from fatigue and depression. As complications of his condition increased, his work performance suffered. He lost his job and his health insurance.

You wouldn't know any of this looking at him. While he seemed to be able to walk okay, standing and all other activities produced consistent discomfort and debilitating pains. These symptoms are consistent with sacroiliac hypermobility and the classic Category II subluxation complex. I offered to send him a sacroiliac (SI) belt, which is designed to hold the loose sacroiliac joints together, like a supportive wrap for a sprained ankle. In cases where the pelvis is particularly unstable, the SI belt becomes an essential companion in the treatment process, helping to accelerate healing. Patients often find a true reduction in their discomfort when wearing an SI belt.

Destitute and disabled, he had no resources to seek additional therapy and was not willing to accept free help. Michael insisted upon being responsible for his situation; however, he could see no way to get the help he needed. A friend of his in the neighborhood was allowing him to live in his basement with his dogs and he did side jobs, mostly painting houses for food, money and other expenses.

He was reluctant to accept my offer but was obviously in need of some help with his condition. I told him that I had a spare SI belt at the office that was unused, and he would be welcome to it. With that explanation, he graciously accepted my offer.

Several weeks passed before I saw him again. He reported that the belt indeed helped considerably while he was wearing it. However, whenever he took it off, the pain immediately returned to the same level.

Hearing this, I knew the sacroiliac joint was overstretched and too loose and was a significant factor in his low back pain. However, even with the support of the belt, the sacroiliac joint was not healing. I recognized this pattern as a Category II subluxation complex in need of proper treatment. I explained a little about the mechanics of the condition that I thought he was suffering from, and how we could possibly help him if he were interested.

Knowing he was reluctant to accept free help, I made Michael a deal. If he would come to my office, I would treat him to see if we could help overcome this devastating condition. In exchange, I would submit bills to the insurance company for the automobile accident, even though his benefits had totally run out. He was comfortable with these conditions and scheduled an appointment.

Upon initial examination, I found mostly what I was expecting. Michael had all the indications of the Category II subluxation complex. Treatments began and Michael responded well, with one exception. He would feel better immediately after a treatment; most of the pain would stop. He was also mostly pain free while he was wearing his SI belt. However, standing and other activities still caused him pain.

Non-stabilization of the pelvis (specifically the Category II subluxation complex) is one indication of DCS, which I treated. However, the problem was not correcting as expected because his symptoms would return treatment after treatment. The treatment was right but additional procedures were needed. For his next visit, additional time was scheduled to perform ISP on Michael.

The full treatment can be safely applied only once a month with very rare exceptions. The extraordinary influx of healing energy and vitality can be overwhelming for the system. If we try to perform too much treatment too quickly, undesirable effects can develop, often in the form of mental and emotional imbalances. While this is not harmful, it is potentially uncomfortable for the patient. In between the full sutural procedures, the other treatments are performed at the rate of one to three times per week.

A companion to the physical effects of these procedures is a generalized enhancement of the overall healing energy and vitality of the person. This isn't just physical energy but also creative and inspirational types of energies. This deeper healing energy can produce effects that the patient may experience as complementary to physical outcomes.

Therefore, when performing ISP, the outcome can be enhanced by identifying and focusing upon a life goal with the patient. By recognizing a deeper intent of the individual, we sometimes lend their heal-

ing systems more power to work toward their bigger life's goal. I spent a few minutes with Michael to identify his life's goal.

I learned that his life's dream was to move to the mountains. He had lived in the Midwest all his life but had always dreamed of living in the Rockies. His current situation — destitute, jobless and without any resources — made this dream seem impossible. Securing transportation to get there with his dogs, finding a job that paid enough to support him and his canine family and sustaining his work in the presence of ongoing pain were high hurdles to scale. Despite his dismal outlook, part of the treatment procedure focused on that goal for his future.

Over the next several months, Michael made slow but steady progress. He physically had less pain for longer periods. His physical energy was slowly returning. A more remarkable transformation was his mood. The depression began to lift almost immediately after the first treatment. Over the next six months, Michael's physical recovery was approximately 80 to 90 percent improved. His stamina increased and his pains were mostly gone.

However, his mental and emotional recoveries were what propelled him forward in life. The depression was gone and his zest for life had returned. Even though Michael lacked the physical resources and guarantees for his future, he still wanted to realize his life's dream. Through the series of treatments for DCS, he regained the motivation and inspiration to take a leap of faith. Against all odds, he packed himself and his dogs and moved to the mountains. His faith in himself had returned as he regained his physical health.

I kept in touch with Michael for over a year after his move. He found a demanding job requiring 70-80-hour workweeks. He successfully *rose to the challenges without reoccurrences of pain or the conditions that previously imposed crippling limitations. I cringe at the thought of what his life would have been like if the severe case of Category II subluxation complex and DCS had not been properly diagnosed and corrected.*

As has been illustrated, DCS does not fully respond to any treatment other than the full cranial sutural procedure, or the enhanced version, the ISP. These specific procedures in Chiropractic Craniopathy require more time, energy and commitment to master than most physicians are willing to undertake. As awareness grows, I am hopeful more chiropractic physicians will become proficient in the specialized procedures in the SOT Methods of Chiropractic and Chiropractic Craniopathy.

Chapter 4

Category II Subluxation Complex and De Jarnette Cranial Syndrome

"The hip bone connected to the …."
– "Dem Bones" by James Weldon Johnson

Anthony and Michael's case studies demonstrate how dysfunction in one part of the body can affect the entire organism. This chapter provides more specifics on the Category II subluxation complex as well as how it triggers DCS.

Category II Subluxation Complex

It all starts in the pelvis. The pelvis is the collection of three major bones: the two hip bones (ilia) and the sacrum or tailbone. In the Category II subluxation, the junction between the sacrum and the hip bone, the Sacroiliac Joint (SIJ), becomes too loose (hypermobile) and slides ever so slightly in a twisting fashion or torsion.

It doesn't take a major catastrophe, as was Anthony's case, to disturb the SIJ. Trauma and other stresses throughout our lives can contribute to turmoil within the sacroiliac joint and a twisting of the hips. These traumas and stresses can originate from birth traumas or even as we are learning to walk. Other stresses, such as mental, emotional, physical, dietary, etc. can damage the SIJ, too. It's important to note that just because a person experiences stresses and traumas, it doesn't mean the Category II system is affected. Problems with the Category II system, however, are quite common.

The Category II subluxation complex begins when the hypermobile SIJ allows one hip to rotate backwards (posterior) and the other to rotate forward (anterior). An exaggerated illustration of this movement is provided in the figure below. This movement sets off a chain reaction of additional imbalances.

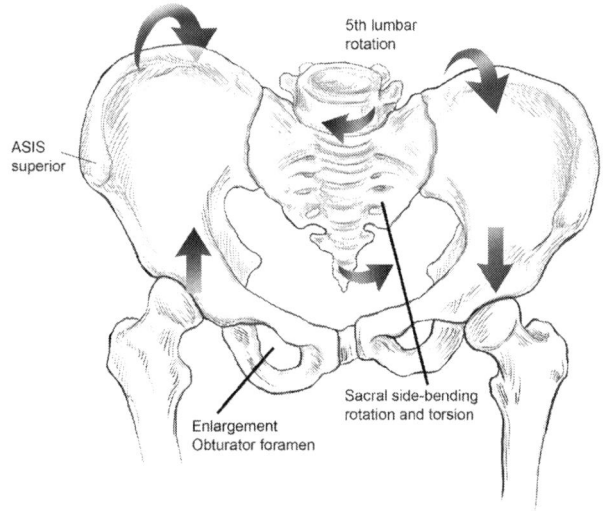

Figure 6: *The Category II subluxation complex produces a collection of mechanical distortions as illustrated. Not only does the pelvis torque, one leg become shorter and the other longer. The fifth lumbar rotates producing greater stresses upon the fifth lumbar disc and an un-level foundation for the rest of the spine that can result in pain, disc issues, scoliosis and many other dysfunctions even affecting the upper body, neck, shoulders and cranium.*

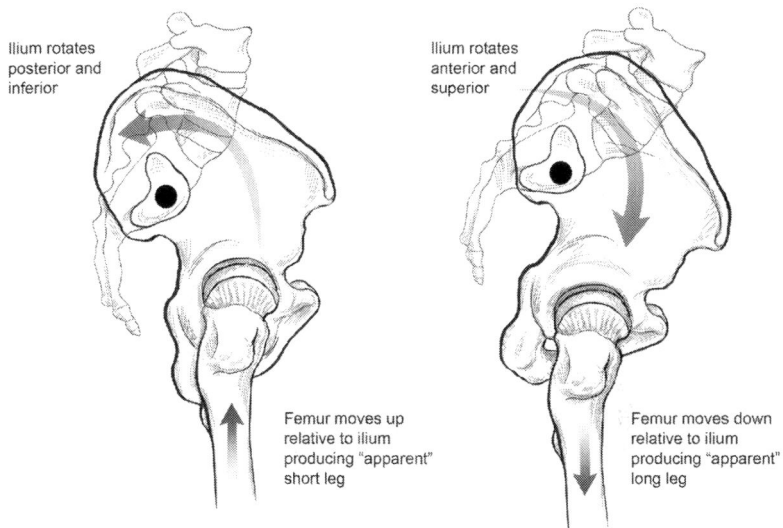

Ilium rotates posterior and inferior

Ilium rotates anterior and superior

Femur moves up relative to ilium producing "apparent" short leg

Femur moves down relative to ilium producing "apparent" long leg

Figure 7: *When the Ilium subluxates it moves around a point of illustration as shown. This in turn produces a force that either pulls the leg bone up or pushes it down. The result is uneven leg lengths that further complicate distortions throughout the body both up the spine to the cranium and down the legs to the feet. One common and overly simplistic approach to this distortion is the use of a heel lift. While this may even out what appears to be unequal leg lengths, it also locks the subluxation complex into place. The preferred approach includes addressing the total Category II subluxation complex.*

When the hip bone rotates, it also affects the hip socket (acetabular cavity) where the leg attaches. When the hip moves backwards, the acetabular cavity moves forward and up (anterior and superior). In compensation, the opposite acetabular cavity moves back and down (posterior and inferior) relative to the posterior hip side.

The result is that one leg is pulled up and the other leg is pushed down. Therefore, when standing, one hip is lower and the other is higher. Just like a poorly designed building, our human building now tilts to the shorter leg side. The effect on the lower body can be swift. When hips twist, they cause a twisting or torsion of the knee and foot. This can lead to pains and other problems in the legs or lower extremities that may eventually affect the foot structure. Foot orthotics may eventually be required to stabilize the pelvis.

The torqueing of the pelvis produces an incredible strain upon the sacral end of the CSRM. When this twisting occurs, it imposes a dampening effect upon the potential innate vitality of the system. In other words, the body may begin to experience a decrease in potential vitality and healing energy. The person may also have low back pain, headaches, neck pain, other body pains or organ dysfunctions because of the strain on the dura.

Significant issues occur above the pelvis, too. To compensate for the shorter leg, the brain, sensing this imbalance, corrects the lean by telling the muscles of the neck and shoulders to tighten up and keep us upright. This correction leads to a new problem — the Category II Distortion Pattern.

The distortion pattern is a major reason why many people constantly experience back and shoulder tension. Any time these biomechanical features of the body's bone structure are out of balance, it will trigger a significant increase in muscle action in the postural muscles of the upper body. If the compensation continues, the brain and neurology are stuck in the habit of producing these muscle tensions. It becomes a reflex, and the person experiencing them can no longer consciously tell those muscles to relax. Many people will complain that they cannot relax the muscles of the neck and shoulders and think that there is something wrong with them. There is, but often the problem begins in the hips.

The problem becomes even more complicated as we move above the neck. In Chapter 3, the reciprocal nature of our bodies was illustrated. A twist of the hips affects the bones in the head. The hip bones (ilia) have a direct connection and relationship with the temporal bones of the skull. When the hip bone rotates (subluxates), the temporal bone on the same side of the body will do the same in the opposite direction.

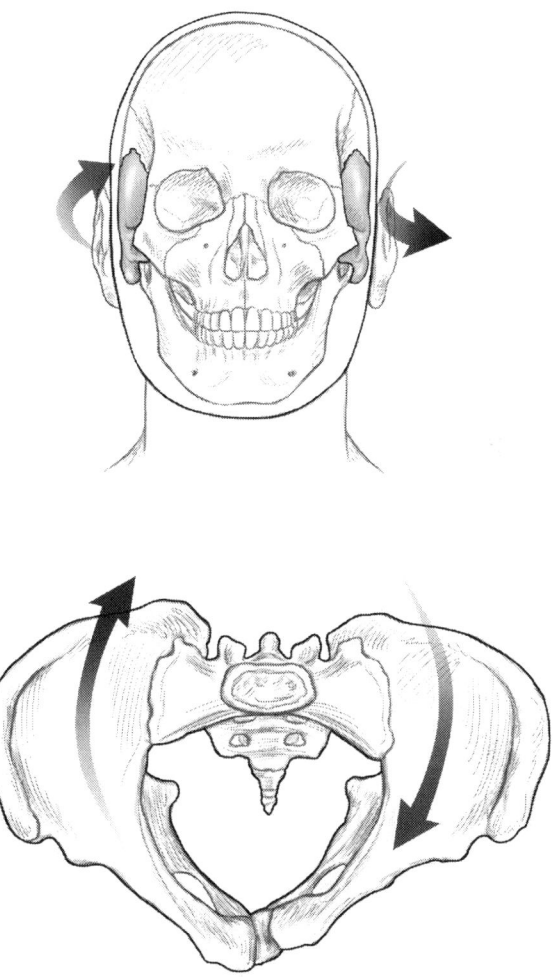

Figure 8: *Cranial Sacral Reciprocity. The reciprocal nature of the bone motions of the occiput and sacrum are well described throughout the history of craniopathy. Another relationship has not received equal attention. That is the reciprocal motion of the Ilium of the hip as it relates to the temporal bone in the cranium. A posteriorly rotated Ilium is accompanied by the internal rotation of the temporal bone on the same side. The anteriorly rotated Ilium is associated with an externally rotated temporal bone on the same side. It should be noted that the pelvic distortions are reflected in the cranium just as cranial distortions are reflected into the pelvis.*

The temporal bone also has a socket much like the hip. The hip socket is for the leg attachment. In the temporal bone, the socket is for the jaw, also known as the mandible, where the bottom teeth sit. This construction creates a hinge, which allows our mouth to open, close, chew, etc. It's attached on each side to the temporal bone in the temporomandibular fossa.

When one hip bone subluxates to the posterior (producing what is called "the short leg side"), the temporal bone on that side will rotate forward, or to the anterior. You will notice in the figure that the jaw joint (condyle of the mandible) is drawn back and down (posterior and inferior). This movement will make the affected side of the jaw less mobile and prevent it from sliding around as much. Left this way, the jaw will become fixated on that side reducing its normal full range of motion.

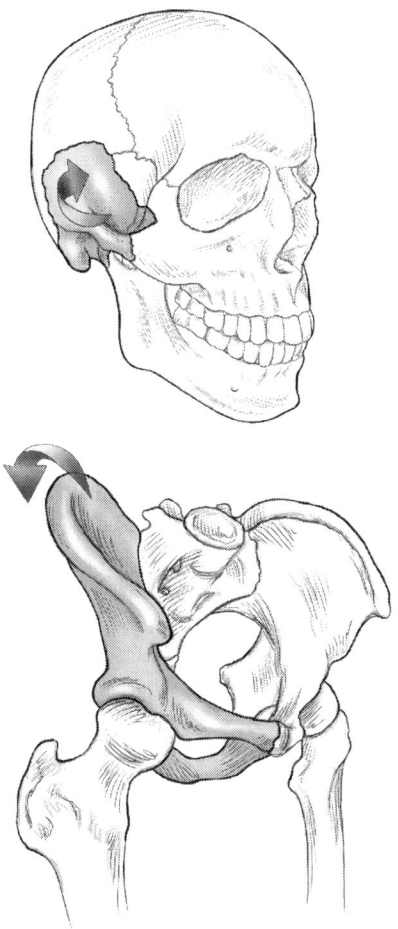

Figure 9: *An internal temporal bone subluxation is associated with the posterior (rotating backwards) Ilium.* **Important note:** *In the Category II subluxation complex, the amount of distortion in the cranium can be measured, sometimes in millimeters. In the normal state, the temporal bones undergo minute internal and external rotation whenever the hip bones move such as with the activity of walking. Furthermore, even the activity of turning one's head engages a minute degree of reciprocal motion of the temporal bones. These motions are in addition to the traditionally described cranial sacral respiratory motions, which are far smaller in amplitude.*

The opposite hip is rotated forward or to the anterior. This pushes the leg down making it seem longer. The temporal bone on that side rotates back and up (posterior and superior). The condyle of the mandible is pushed forward, and the temporomandibular fossa is more open. The jawbone (mandible) on this side becomes looser and moves around more. This increased motion produces irritation and inflammation, making this side of the jaw more susceptible to injury and trauma, as well as wear and tear.

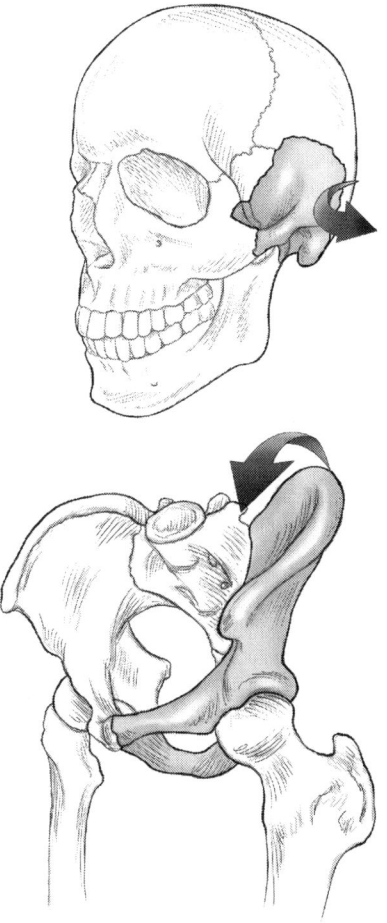

Figure 10: *The subluxation of an Ilium as it rotates to the front (anterior) is accompanied by an external rotation of the temporal bone on the same side of the body.*

It is this pushed up and forward movement that can cause temporomandibular dysfunction (TMD). The Category II subluxation complex will often result in temporomandibular joint (TMJ) pains, dysfunctions and other problems.

The twisting doesn't end at the jaw. The occiput, underneath the temporal bones, becomes twisted. One side of the occiput is pushed down (inferior) and the other side is pulled upward (superior). This results in a wedging effect upon the Atlas or top vertebra (C-1) of the spine, pushing it out to one side and back. In chiropractic, this is referred to as the posterior Atlas subluxation.

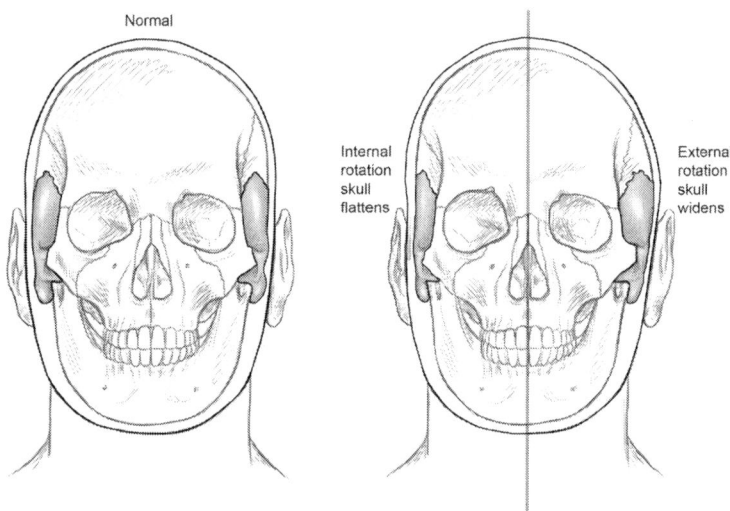

Figure 11: *A common subluxation pattern in the cranium is the reciprocal internal/external distortion of the cranial bones that corresponds to the pelvic twist of the Category II subluxation complex, resulting in the De Jarnette Cranial Syndrome. In the cranial portion of this subluxation complex, one side of the head will appear narrower and the opposite will widen. It is thought that this portion of the cranial structures may result in alteration of the cerebral spinal fluid flow patterns in the brain, intracranial pressure and distortion of the passageways for the cranial nerves.*

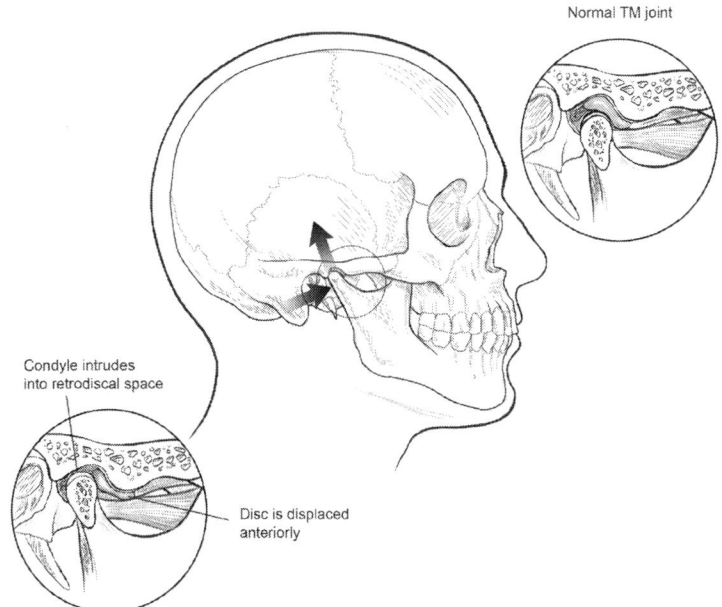

Normal TM joint

Condyle intrudes
into retrodiscal space

Disc is displaced
anteriorly

Figure 12: *This depicts the relative malposition of the jaw with respect to the external temporal bone. This shift in position may lead to hypermobility and a displacement of the TMJ disk. Eventually this can lead to temporomandibular joint dysfunction, popping, clicking, pain and other dysfunctions.*

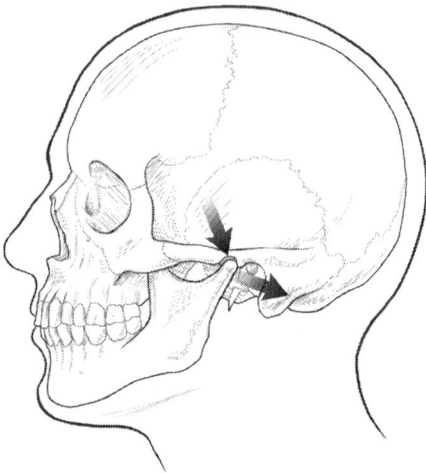

Figure 13: *Just as a subluxation of the Ilium in the pelvis alters the relative leg lengths, the resulting temporal bone subluxations repositions the part of the temporal bones that hold the jaw. This figure depicts the altered position of the jaw in relationship to the internal temporal bone subluxation. The condyle of the jaw can be somewhat restricted and therefore results in a reduction of normal motion.*

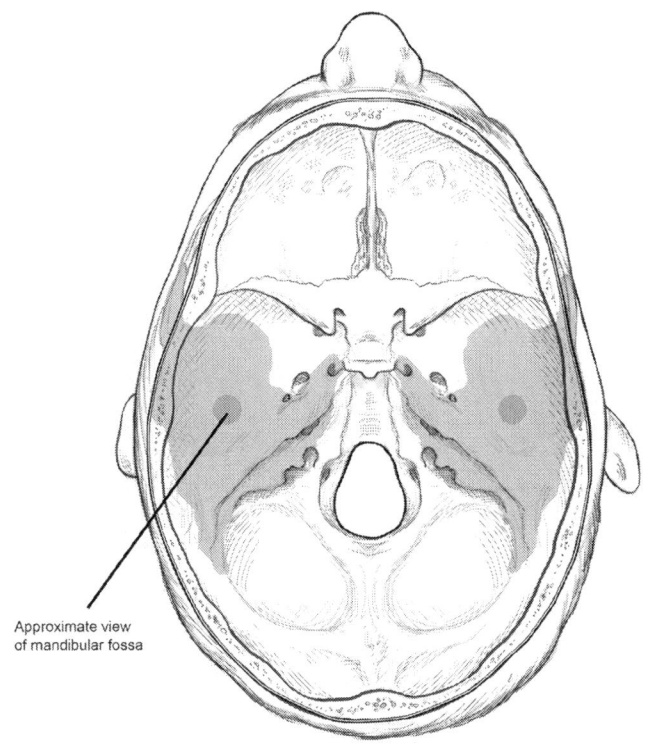

Approximate view
of mandibular fossa

Figure 14: *This top view through the skull demonstrates the position of the mandibular condyle, the part of the jaw that fits into the skull.*

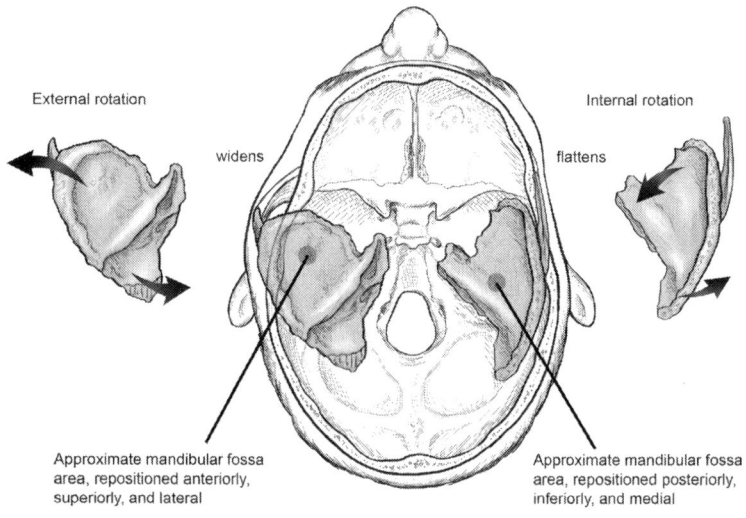

External rotation

widens

Internal rotation

flattens

Approximate mandibular fossa area, repositioned anteriorly, superiorly, and lateral

Approximate mandibular fossa area, repositioned posteriorly, inferiorly, and medial

Figure 15: *The cranial distortion of the Category II subluxation complex and the resulting De Jarnette Cranial Syndrome alters the relative position of the jaw joint as shown here. These subluxations often result in temporomandibular joint dysfunction (TMD) as well as a host of other negative effects upon the brain and its many functions.*

The Axis or second vertebra of the cervical spine (C-2) will cause a posterior rotation of C-2 on the opposite side of the posterior Atlas.

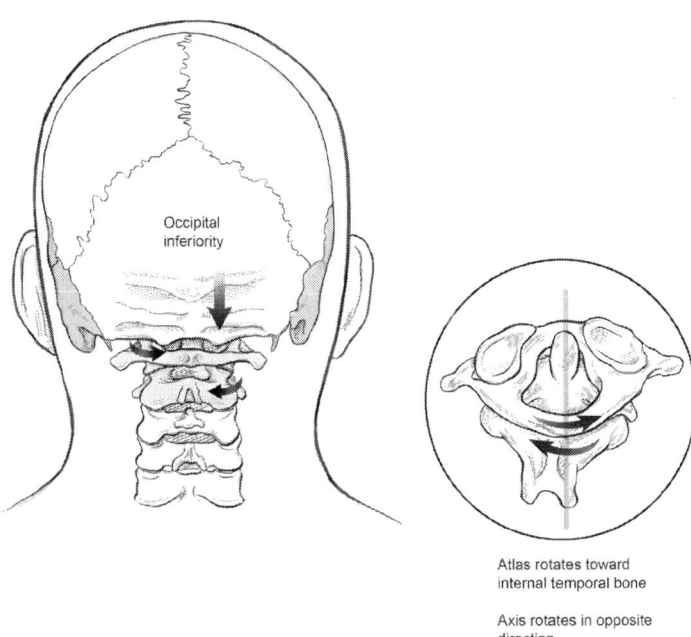

Occipital
inferiority

Atlas rotates toward
internal temporal bone

Axis rotates in opposite
direction

Figure 16: *The Category II subluxation of the pelvis produces a dropping of the sacrum on the short leg side and the accompanying drop in the occiput of the cranium. This in turn adds a force into the top vertebra of the spine (Atlas) pushing it to the opposite side. The second cervical vertebra (axis) then counter rotates to the opposite direction. These subluxations of the upper cervical spine are thought to impede cerebral spinal fluid flow out of the brain causing an increased intracranial pressure leading to a host of health complications. Some practitioners focus only on the upper cervical end of this subluxation complex addressing only the position of the Atlas. In the Sacro Occipital Technic of chiropractic and Chiropractic Craniopathy the entire system is viewed as important and integrated. Interventions are directed throughout the entire body and has required to relieve stresses and distortions that affect the total subluxation complex.*

The summation of all these twisting forces results in a torqueing subluxation of the entire cranial structure. Each of the bones plays a part in the overall torsion of the cranium. The dura responds to all the twisting by also torqueing. Now the entire spine is involved.

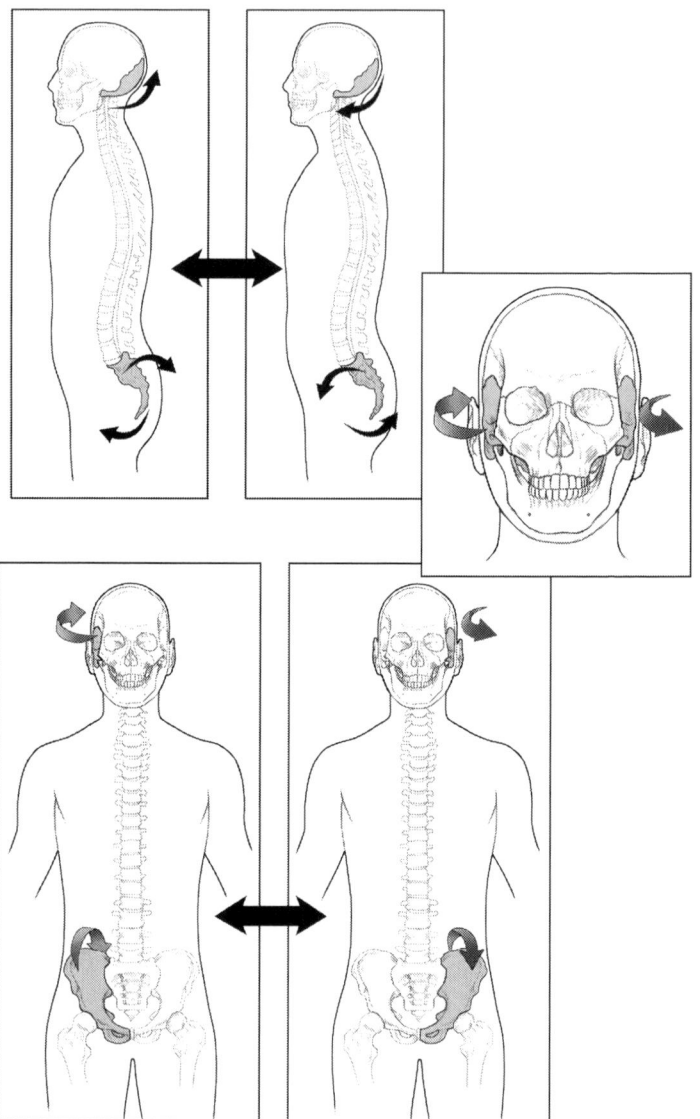

Figure 17: *The cranium, pelvis, dura and all its attachments form the cranial sacral respiratory mechanism (CSRM). This mechanism is described as moving in a cyclical fashion through the body and is described as the motions of flexion and extension.*

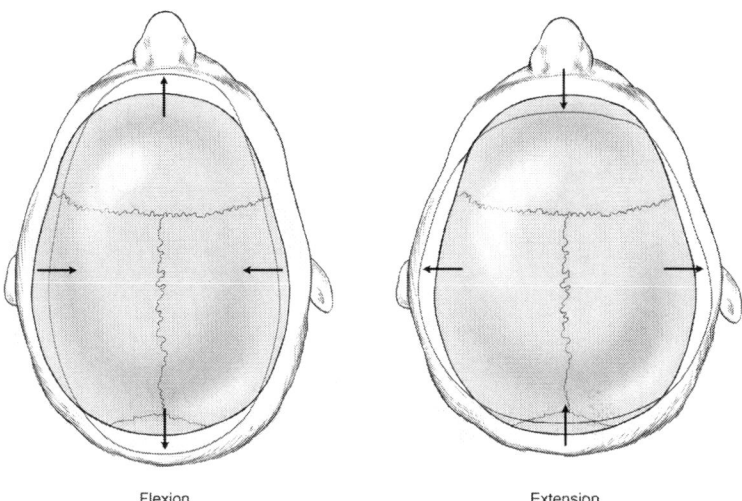

Flexion

Extension

Figure 18: *This figure illustrates the motion in extreme flexion as well as extreme extension from the cranial perspective. In the Category II subluxation complex, the torsional forces in the pelvis and cranium often produce a relative state of extension on one side of the cranium and flexion on the other due to the reciprocal relationship of the temporal bones. The subluxation complex results in the observed cranial asymmetry illustrated in some of the research studies.*

The overall distortion complex produces several disturbing effects to the head and brain. Inside the brain, the mechanism constantly producing CSF comes under pressure as escape routes for the CSF are compressed. Kept under pressure for too long or in a chronic state can negatively affect brain function.

Some researchers are currently hypothesizing that this kind of backup in brain pressure from the CSF may be implicated in such diseases as Alzheimer's, Parkinson's, Multiple Sclerosis, Dementia and other problems. Practitioners of Chiropractic Craniopathy often report clinical experience suggesting that these pressures can cause a multitude of symptoms and complaints anywhere in the body.

Another source of potential alterations in brain function results from the twisting of the dural membranes. The design of the dural membranes produces various compartments in the cranium. Twists and distortions in the structures may alter pressures from one section of the brain to another. This may also result in a lack of proper coordination between the different parts of the brain, which can lead to other issues.

It may sound cliché, but a ripple in the hip bones can cause a cascade of problems in the head.

Case Study - Sarah

I first saw Sarah when she was 53 years of age. At that time, her major complaint was neck pains of two to three months' duration. As we investigated her condition further, she also described shoulder pains of approximately 10 years' duration. She had a loss of cartilage that supplementation with glucosamine didn't help. She had experienced low back pain off and on for years along with plantar fasciitis of an intermittent nature.

In addition, hot flashes had been problematic for a couple of years and stomach pains and general gastritis were frequent occurrences. Nutritional intervention and general chiropractic had helped to some extent over the previous month, but all her problems persisted.

Sarah lived quite a distance away. To complicate matters, she traveled considerably for business. Despite her rugged schedule and long distance to travel for treatment, I was able to see her 12 times over the first three months. Her recovery during this time was somewhat rocky. At one point, she had a significant reoccurrence of the severe low back pain. It lasted a couple of weeks, and then it resolved nicely. It's common for a body that has been compensating for a distortion to fight to remain in a compensatory state versus adapting to and maintaining the proper alignment after treatment.

While body parts can get out of alignment from sudden trauma or stresses, imbalances can also develop slowly over time, such as an adult who at age two hit his head, which resulted in a cranial subluxation affecting his balance. Our bodies are skilled at adapting and compensating for problems, meaning a condition can progress for years without any symptoms or pains. Finally, when the body can't tolerate any further disturbance, symptoms emerge. This is why we have reports of individuals experiencing severe low back pain by simply bending over to pick up a golf ball. What feels sudden to the golfer has really been developing for many years.

To further confuse the issue, when the first symptom shows up it is often distant from the real problem not only in timing, but also in location. For example, neck pain and headaches may be caused from an imbalance or subluxation in the pelvis. The low back or hips may not hurt but the neck and head do.

To correct the problem behind the neck and head pains, the pelvis must be rebalanced. Over the years that this subluxation complex has developed, various muscles, ligaments and other structural compensations have become fixated in abnormal stress patterns. If this is the case, once the subluxation complex is corrected, the patient may experience a period of low back pain and discomfort as the body adapts to its proper balance.

Despite of all the factors that inhibited ideal healing, Sarah was doing better. It was eventually determined that SIJ hypermobility or Category II subluxation complex was at the root of her issues. It was recommended she start wearing a sacroiliac belt and performing certain stabilizing exercises. Along with the pelvic balancing of the Category II subluxation, specific cranial suture subluxations were addressed.

At the end of three months, her low back pain was much better. She could endure long, grueling trips without severe incident. She could not perform heavy exercise yet, but the improvement in the low back was remarkable. However, what was most noteworthy about Sarah's situation was the neck pain was also completely gone, along with the shoulder pain, plantar fasciitis and gastritis. Treating the Category II subluxation complex alone completely resolved all these other symptoms.

This case illustrates how the healing mechanism is constructed. The stresses produced by the Category II subluxation complex and the sutural fixations inhibited how the body functioned physiologically and neurologically, impeding a primary component of the healing mechanism. Even though the body heals itself, the Category II subluxation and the DCS can't heal on their own and instead must be addressed by a trained chiropractic physician.

We are led to believe that treatment is determined first by a proper diagnosis of the symptoms and then the application of counteracting measures to address the local issues. With a Category II subluxation complex and sutural fixations, the cause of a problem is not always in the same location as the symptoms. Maintaining a curious and open mind as to the causes of the symptoms usually leads to a satisfactory conclusion because healing occurs when we restore the system's ability to function normally. The primary malfunction addressed in Sarah was the Category II subluxation complex and the associated cranial dysfunction.

By enabling this mechanism in Sarah, structural balance was improved. Pressure was alleviated from spinal nerves allowing the brain to efficiently send its healing messages throughout the entire structure. The

CSRM could pump CSF more efficiently through the spinal canal. CSF pressure was reduced in the brain, and coordination of healing efforts and structural functions were improved.

The SOT Methods of Chiropractic enable the body to heal itself by correcting the mechanisms the body uses to run neurological systems normally. The doctor does not have to address every little problem but must treat the right things. Correct the problem and you have only helped the problem. Correct the whole body, and the problems heal themselves.

De Jarnette Cranial Syndrome

To complicate matters, trauma or chronic Category II subluxations can result in restriction of the joint system (sutures) throughout the skull. When motion is decreased or lost in the cranial bones, the CSF pump is compromised, and additional pressures build inside the cranium. As noted previously, this condition is the De Jarnette Cranial Syndrome (DCS).

DCS involves every bone in the cranium because the joints between the bones are not able to move properly. This loss of movement means the bones can't adequately perform the essential action of CSF pumping. DCS also affects the dural system but is not a primary dura subluxation. There are three major parts of the cranial mechanisms: the dura; the Category II sutural system; and the rhythmical motions of the cranial sacral pump. When the sutural system subluxates, it affects the entire structure and can produce relatively large distortions in the cranial alignment.

Because of these sizable mechanical alterations, other structures of the head, such as the cranial foramen, may become affected. The foramina are the tiny holes the cranial nerves pass through. If head bones are twisted, some of these little holes may become misshapen and the nerves that go through these holes can become compressed. The pressure created by the compression can change the functional ability of the afflicted nerves, causing problems for the patient. The result may be pain or muscle spasm or other kinds of problems, such as trigeminal neuralgia, a condition resulting in pain and, at times, muscle twitching of the face. The illustration below is taken from a real human skull. Note the difference in the sizes of the foramen marked by the arrows on either side. They are clearly not the same size.

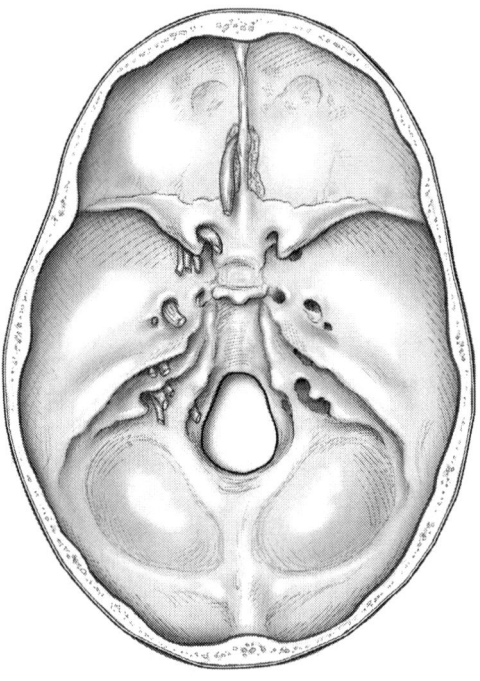

Figure 19: *Inside the cranial bones are 12 pair of holes (called foramen) that provide exits for the cranial nerves. These nerves control much of the critical functions of the head and upper body.*

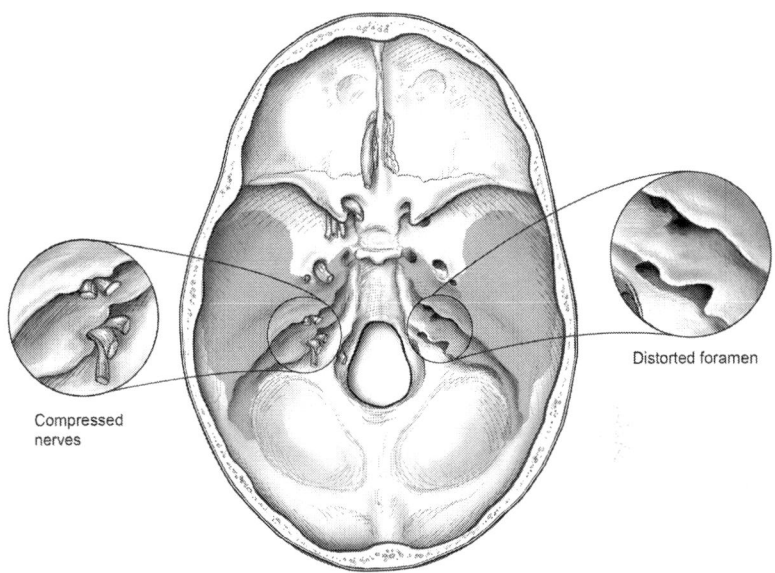

Compressed
nerves

Distorted foramen

Figure 20: *Cranial subluxations can produce pressures on some of the cranial nerves. These cranial distortions can be the result of the Category II subluxation complex and the resulting De Jarnette Cranial Syndrome (DCS). Conditions such as Trigeminal Neuralgia and Temporomandibular Dysfunction, and others, may result.*

It is important to understand that these stresses are also a part of a safety mechanism for the pelvis. The cranial sutures can allow only so much movement. This prevents the dura from becoming more stressed and reciprocally prevents the pelvis from twisting further. The specific area of concern is the pelvis. SIJ has no muscle crossing it to lend structural support. It has surrounding muscles essential for pelvic motions, but the ligaments of the sacroiliac joint itself is a lone crusader with respect to gravitational support of the body.

While your brain neurologically compensates for this dysfunction, a structural mechanism that limits the amount of damage that can occur, due to the Category II subluxation complex, is sutural locking. Sutural locking provides an essential health maintenance mechanism but, at the same time, robs us of vitality and often causes neurological dysfunction from the brain to various parts of the body.

When the sutures become fixed, as in the DCS, the ramifications can be swift, painful and debilitating, as demonstrated in the following case study.

Case Study – Nick

The cranium affords protection of the brain from outside forces and has shock absorber qualities. This is why we can receive a hit on the head and even suffer a concussion, but we recover without negative effects.

While on a trip to Germany, Nick received a minor shock to his head. The blow was so incidental that he carried on with his day as if it hadn't happened. It wasn't the first time he'd been hit in the head. This time his body responded differently.

Within one to two hours, a series of cascading sensations wracked his body. Each sensation seemed to be triggered by the one before, just like falling dominoes. Soon there were pains along his entire right side. His neck, shoulder, hip, knee, foot and ankle all developed discomforts.

The symptoms persisted and had an almost a crippling effect. Over time, his right foot changed physical shape and a visible dropping of the arch and other contours in the foot and ankle appeared. Nick pursued treatments from a variety of doctors around the world. Nothing helped.

I first saw him at the age of 45, seven years after his minor bump on the head. He was in a state of constant discomfort. He didn't use a wheelchair or crutches, but it was obvious his right side was impaired.

He had lost sensation in his right foot, leaving him feeling as if it didn't touch the ground. He couldn't lift himself using only his right foot muscles. His inability to do this simple act was a sign of a possible neurological problem.

Nick's structures and functions were analyzed, issues were identified in various parts of the spine and pelvis and were treated accordingly. The right-sided symptoms improved. Unfortunately, the positive changes were brief. Nick would feel a reduction in his problems for a few days at best. Over the next two months, his symptoms improved and then deteriorated a few days later with each treatment. I had no doubt that Nick's issues could be resolved, but I still didn't know how to accomplish it.

Because Nick had received cranial adjustments from many of the top experts around the world, and his body had responded poorly to previous treatments, I didn't consider a full sutural adjustment. After months of positive results only to see him regress into pain again, I re-evaluated him and decided to perform the full cranial sutural procedure (ISP).

Nick could perform a partial calf raise immediately following the first treatment. His leg muscle was beginning to work again, and he felt sensations in his right foot that confirmed it was touching the ground. Over the next few weeks, he reported a 20 to 25 percent improvement overall. It was confirmed. Nick suffered from the DCS.

A second full cranial sutural procedure was performed about a month later with dramatic results. Initially he reported about an 80 percent improvement of symptoms. This level of improvement didn't last long, but it settled to a respectable 50 to 60 percent improvement over the following month.

I was curious as to how the minor incident from seven years earlier could result in such an intense reaction that nearly crippled him. I learned that Nick grew up in the country and was quite active in his younger years. He experienced many physical traumas, especially head injuries. He recounted numerous falls off horses, hay bales and injuries from sporting activities. There were elbows to the head and many concussions. Young and strong, none of these slowed him down much. The injuries seemed to heal, and he had no residual side effects until his trip to Germany.

Repeated injuries and traumas had taken their toll, but his body had adapted and compensated for those stresses. The head bump in Germany proved to be the "straw that broke the camel's back." His body, accepting and recovering from blow after blow, could no longer adapt. It responded by breaking down.

Which is why we must always look beyond the simple and immediate circumstances of an injury, as even a small impact can trigger a much larger event, resulting in dramatic consequences. Nick and many others demonstrate this.

Another full sutural procedure was performed. Nick is still under treatment as of this writing, but I fully expect him to make a complete recovery. This may require several more treatments over the coming months, but eventual success is almost certain. Because of his history of multiple and serious traumas, the complete correction will take longer. Treatment in this case is correcting decades of serious and cumulative cranial subluxations.

Temporomandibular Joint Dysfunction (TMD)

As mentioned earlier, another common problem is temporomandibular joint dysfunction (TMD). It is thought that TMD very often results from the distortions produced by DCS. Virtually every person suffering from DCS has some degree of temporomandibular joint dysfunction. It may not be causing any pains or problems, but imbalances are likely to be present. Another jaw-related problem is bruxism or teeth grinding. It's believed that teeth grinding is the body's attempt to reduce the stress caused by immobile head sutures. Bruxism is a consistent indicator of the DCS and, left untreated, can cause significant dental issues.

Long-term DCS tends to cause increased levels of tension in the jaw muscles, as well as the upper neck and sides of head. Part of the full sutural procedure, ISP, is aimed at alleviating the DCS by directly addressing increased muscular tension of the entire upper body region, as well as the muscles of the jaw and the rest of the cranium.

For those suffering from headaches, TMD or bruxism, the pelvic subluxations will need to be addressed before the problems in the head can totally resolve. Likewise, if lower back pain, leg problems, disc disease, sciatica, etc. is present, it may be necessary to normalize the function of the cranial sutures before the lower body problems can be resolved.

Brain Trauma

Traumatic Brain Injury (TBI) is a common cause of the DCS. TBIs can also be called concussion, post-concussive syndrome (PCS), neuronal injuries, mild brain injury, shaken baby syndrome and others.

Closed-head injury is a type of traumatic brain injury in which the skull and dura mater remain intact. The Centers for Disease Control (CDC) tracks closed head injuries as reported by hospital emergency room data. Cases that go unreported or are treated by a private physician aren't included. According to the CDC in its *Guide to Writing about Traumatic Brain Injury in News and Social Media (2015):*

- In 2010, 2.5 million emergency department (ED) visits, hospitalizations or deaths were related to TBI, either alone or in combination with other injuries, in the United States.
- TBI contributed to the deaths of over 50,000 people.
- TBI-related ED visits for sports- and recreation-related injuries increased 62 percent from 153,375 in 2001 to 248,418 in 2009 among persons aged 19 or younger.
- The total cost of ED visits, hospitalizations and deaths related to TBIs, either alone or in combination with other injuries, exceeded $82 billion annually, including medical and productivity loss costs.

That dollar figure doesn't include factors such as pain and suffering. Many of the injured never fully recover and pay a lifetime of consequences. The true cost to society and individuals is certainly much higher than these conservative estimates from the CDC.

Imagine how much of that $82 billion could possibly be saved by Chiropractic Craniopathy once the true emergency nature of the situation is resolved. Far too often, the suffering continues long after the traditional treatments have reached their limits of effectiveness. Proper research would greatly enhance our ability to treat head injury victims.

Case Study – Daniel

Daniel was a 17-year-old high school football player. During a routine play, he dove for the ball and met the opposition. The impact was brutal. It forced his head backwards and cracked his helmet. Immediately, he noticed pain in his left low back.

He developed a large bump on his forehead that day, but it went away quickly. Daniel was evaluated for any signs of a concussion, but none was found. Being young, healthy and strong, everyone assumed Dan-

iel would get over his pains in a couple of days. After all, football play-ers suffer aches and pains constantly.

His initial symptoms included some numbness on the skin of his left leg and pain in his low back that changed when he turned his head. He developed headaches easily, whereas he hadn't had them before. As time went on, Daniel experienced ongoing stiffness in his neck, as well as his upper and lower back. He felt tired all the time. To complicate matters even further, he also developed insomnia. He couldn't get the rest he needed. He also described a strange and generalized tension in his head that never went away and worsened at night.

Constantly in pain and frustrated at the lack of answers from his doc-tors, Daniel visited my office. Because of the severity of his injury, an x-ray examination of his low back and neck was taken to be sure there were no broken bones or other dangerous conditions that would prevent safe treatment. Minor misalignments were found in various areas of the spine, but nothing in any of the traditional examinations explained all his symptoms.

In the absence of a clear cause of his pain and suffering, we began a series of trial treatments to determine the best plan to resolve his injuries. His progress proved discouraging. Treatment would provide some relief leading us to believe we were on the right track; however, his condition was never fully resolved. Because he lived quite a dis-tance from the clinic and had a full high school schedule of classes and activities, he was unable to visit often. He came when he could. Daniel was seen 13 times over the next four years without major progress. We tried almost everything. He religiously performed therapeutic exercises and stretches. He underwent physical therapy with the hope it would alleviate his symptoms, but the problems continued. He elected to try other therapeutic approaches, so I didn't see Daniel for several years.

When he returned to resume treatment, it had almost been 10 years since the initial injury. Daniel had graduated from college and had moved closer to the clinic. Time had not been kind to his body. He had developed pain in his knees and the bottoms of his feet would "burn" and feel numb when running. These new symptoms were added to the list of those he already had. He was still having difficulty sleeping and continuously suffered from the head pressure that started immediately following the football injury.

The symptoms would seem to get better at times but would never go away. Now they had become worse again and even his face felt tight. Treatments over the next year or so seemed to help some but offered only minor relief. We were performing traditional treatments to balance his spine and pelvis as well as performing various cranial adjustments. He would feel better for a day or two, sometimes longer, and steady progress was being made. I wasn't convinced we had found the root of his problem, yet still believed he could become asymptomatic and permanently recover from this condition. However, since he wasn't achieving total results, Daniel took another break from treatment.

He came back again after nearly 12 years out from his original injury. While his symptoms had lessened for a while after our last series of treatments, they did eventually return. His head and neck pains had worsened considerably for no apparent reason.

I was more determined than ever to find the underlying cause of Daniel's issues. I began to wonder if Daniel's cranial structures had fixated to the point that no other treatment except ISP would resolve these issues. Could he possibly be suffering from DCS? In a consultation, I described the full cranial sutural treatment process and why I believed this could be what he needed to make permanent progress in his condition. He agreed to a series of the full sutural procedures.

Daniel felt significant improvements after the first session. The head pressure disappeared for several days and his headaches diminished. It appeared we were on the right track. After three treatments, the results were meeting our expectations. All his symptoms had completely resolved. He could run again, and the headaches were gone. The back tension and pain went away, and his feet didn't hurt anymore. He finally realized complete relief from the effects of a traumatic head injury that plagued him daily for over 12 years. Today, his traumatic high school injury is only a memory, as he remains symptom-free.

The experience with Daniel heightens the awareness of DCS for other sufferers. How many others suffer for years, if not their entire lives, with DCS? How much pain, suffering and medical expenses could be spared by using these noninvasive protocols? We will only get answers to these questions with adequate research.

Cranial trauma can be devastating. It also can be persistent and unrelenting, not treatable by any conventional methods. For sufferers from DCS, the full cranial sutural procedure may well be the only effective treatment. If all else has failed, Chiropractic Craniopathy may be the answer. Daniel's recovery illustrates this concept beautifully.

Stroke

A cerebrovascular accident (CVA), sometimes called a cerebrovascular insult (CVI), is usually referred to simply as a stroke. This is a condition that occurs in the brain that can have effects ranging from mild to fatal. There are two major ways that this occurs. One is that some blockage prevents blood flow to a portion of the brain. An example of this would be a blood clot or some sort of a block that prevents blood flow from that point into the areas of the brain supplied by that artery. The second would be a rupture in a blood vessel, which would also produce a lack of blood flow.

In either case, the essential element is lack of oxygen. Within a very short time, the area of the brain that is not getting enough of this precious gas to function normally, literally dies. If it is a very tiny portion, the incident may go completely unnoticed. If it is large enough, it can cause numerous symptoms, depending upon exactly where in the brain it occurs. If it is in the speech center, the patient's ability to speak suffers in varying degrees. If it is in a center that controls muscle function to an arm or leg, then the ability to use that limb is compromised or lost. If the memory area is damaged, that function will be lost, etc.

Worldwide, stroke is the second largest cause of death. In 2010, approximately 7 million individuals suffered from a stroke and over 6 million of those were fatal. Currently, at least 30 million people worldwide suffer the effects of previous strokes. The financial toll in the United States alone was estimated to be over $70 billion in medical costs. This does not consider the devastation to families and lives, as well as loss of productivity and income.

Stroke is a very serious medical condition and can often be prevented with proper diet and other preventative measures. The staggering statistics alone should be sufficient to motivate people to take appropriate preventative measures. It would behoove everyone to learn to recognize the signs of a stroke and treat it for what it is: a medical emergency. Fortunately, medical science has made great strides in minimizing the effects of this type of condition - if caught early. Prevention and timely treatment are paramount.

Another cause of stroke can be genetic predisposition. Our bodies are preprogrammed by our genes. Every detail, such as a freckle or the shape of a hand and foot, is influenced by the blueprints contained in our genetic makeup. The exact design of every millimeter of the blood vessel system can be traced back to the precise genetic blueprint. If there is some flaw in the blueprint, a weak spot in a blood vessel may occur. If this area is in the brain, that person may be more susceptible to events, such as a stroke. If an affected vessel is close to the skin, that person may frequently find what appears to be broken blood vessels in that area.

Traumatic injury or other events that can cause a weakness in an artery or vein can also cause a stroke.

Most strokes are preventable if one undertakes the proper measures. Still, even with the best diet and health habits, a cerebral vascular accident can occur unexpectedly. Such was the case with Ryan.

Case Study: Ryan

Ryan was a robust, health-conscious individual with extraordinary mentally acuity. As an illustration of his mental capacity he designed every detail of his 4000 sq. ft. home... in his head! Of course, blueprints had to be produced for the builders, but they were absolutely amazed at his capacity to design and redesign the thousands of details in his head. Ryan was not a designer, architect or builder. He was a salesman by trade with an obviously brilliant mind.

Then one day something felt wrong, and he decided to make a trip to the emergency room. Tests were administered; however, no dysfunction was identified. He was released and sent home. A day passed and the symptoms escalated. This time he was admitted to the hospital and was found to have suffered a massive stroke. Its severity was critical enough to warrant an emergency helicopter trip to a facility more equipped to handle his condition.

When I was initially contacted, questions loomed large as to whether he would even survive this massive trauma. Fortunately, he did pull through, but the neurologist informed him and the family that he would never walk or speak again. The damage to his brain was medically permanent and extensive. The prospects were grim, and the family was devastated. Everyone was thankful that he was alive, but the loss of productivity by such a brilliant soul, stricken at the age of 57, was difficult to contemplate.

I had known Ryan for many years and witnessed his body's ability to respond to previous traumas and conditions with amazing resilience. I felt deep down that he could indeed recover from this setback to a much greater degree than was being medically predicted. I also knew that he and his wife were of superior mental attitude and strong faith, which can be significant contributors to any healing process. All these elements contributed to the astounding healing progress described below.

Ryan was speechless and barely able to move around, so I knew the sooner we could initiate the process, the better it would be for his ultimate prospects. After discharge from the hospital, he and his wife stopped by my office on their way home to pick up the nutritional program I recommended to help assist the healing process in these situations. I wanted him to begin an active treatment program immediately.

Physically devastated, he was not able to come in for treatment for several months; however, he did engage in the nutritional protocol for brain inflammation and rehabilitation. He felt that it was helping significantly and began to experience improvement at a rate thought to be impossible, medically. Still, his problems were nowhere near resolved.

After he had recovered enough to travel, Ryan began a treatment regimen at my office. One of the prominent features of his treatment program was Chiropractic Craniopathy, in order to facilitate cerebral spinal fluid flow and assure healing energy got to the brain. Areas of the brain that were damaged by the stroke obviously could not be returned to normal function, but sometimes in these situations, other areas of the brain can learn to take over the lost functions.

We had no idea if Ryan was capable of this type of transference because his damage was so extensive. But as soon as we applied the specialized techniques in Chiropractic Craniopathy to facilitate this process, his response was immediate and encouraging. Over the course of the next year, he continued to improve dramatically, albeit with the expected ups and downs. It was not smooth or easy, more like a roller-coaster ride.

Speech increasingly became easier, and his pain levels decreased. His weakened arm and leg began working more normally again. Over the next 12-18 months all outward signs of the stroke had virtually disappeared. Any person observing Ryan would not have been able to tell that he had any previous disabilities.

However, Ryan began believing that the nutritional and Chiropractic Craniopathy treatments had reached a plateau. His description was that it felt as if a portion of his brain function was not there yet; that is, the ability to conceptualize and create thoughts and ideas had something of a hole, a missing piece. With our other measures having reached a plateau of effectiveness, we added a regime of AlphaBio Centrix (ABC) energy healing patches. The effects were virtually immediate. Within a couple of days both Ryan and his wife were noticing astounding changes. SOT® Chiropractic and Chiropractic Craniopathy treatments continued in order to assure optimal brain function as well as spinal, leg and arm functions. When we added the ABC protocols, all improvements escalated dramatically. I knew we were on the right track when the couple reported that they found themselves laughing again: an activity that had been in short supply since the stroke.

These additional energetic treatments continued for several months, but Ryan still reported a bit of a missing space in his head. As he continued to live with his situation and interact with the world around him, he came to realize that part of what was missing in his brain were his normal feelings.

As noted earlier, this was a massive stroke. It affected the parietal area of the brain which controls the ability of body parts to move. It also affected a large area of the frontal region which has influence over things like speech, memory and feelings. Ryan was missing his emotions. We continued to adjust some of the details of the treatment program until we happened upon a new and effective combination.

For a few days he felt as if some of these functions were turned on and back to normal. This did not stay immediately fixed, but the feedback we received directed our course of action for the next few months. Currently this is an ongoing treatment process.

While Ryan is not back to 100%. he estimates he is at about 90%+ of his original function. He only has 10% to go at this report! I have faith that the additional 10% will return. As we approach the two-year anniversary of a life-threatening situation that was predicted to cost him his speech and mobility for the rest of his life, the changes are nothing short of miraculous.

How does one recover from a life-threatening stroke to become virtually normal again? Watching Ryan's progression compels me to imagine how other people suffering similarly might benefit from cutting-edge, non-traditional treatments and strategies. An exciting prospect indeed! I also ask why these strategies are not utilized by mainstream medicine?

I did obtain some insights by working with Ryan.

His doctors at a big medical Center here in St. Louis were absolutely dumbfounded and amazed at his progress. They asked if he would be willing to present himself for some tests so that they could begin to understand how his healing process was so spectacular. He agreed on one condition: that his treating physician accompany him for the testing. The medical doctors at the hospital readily agreed and were most excited to discover what this doctor had done for Ryan.

All parties were excited and interested in what they may learn. Arrangements for testing were begun. Then the investigators asked Ryan who the doctor was so they could contact him or her for the testing. When they found out that his primary treating doctor was a chiropractic physician, they instantly lost all interest in the project.

This simply illustrates that much of the research that results in treatment procedures for ailing patients specifically ignores treatments that fall outside the standard mainstream beliefs. As they say, "If you always do what you have always done you will always get what you have always gotten."

Therefore, it is not surprising that many treatments and therapies will not be recommended by your mainstream healthcare professionals. It is often said that these treatments are unproven because they have not undergone the scrutiny of scientific investigation. There is a serious problem in that alternative treatments are automatically excluded from investigational processes. In other words, things that get the research are the things that are already popular. This double-bind situation creates a barrier to conducting research on treatments and protocols that fall "outside the current medical box," even though there are demonstrated successes, such as Ryan's.

One more truly important element in Ryan's recovery. He took charge of his healthcare and self-directed the therapies that enabled his miraculous recovery. When people can take a more active role in their healthcare decision-making process, their recovery process is energized. Given the right opportunity, positive support and relentless encouragement, even an injured mind can help heal itself.

Chapter 5
Cranial Distortion

"We are accustomed to look for the gross and immediate effect and to ignore all else. Unless this appears promptly, we deny the existence of hazard. Even research men suffer from the handicap of inadequate methods of detecting the beginnings of injury. The lack of sufficiently delicate methods to detect injury before symptoms appear is one of the great unsolved problems in medicine."

– Rachel Carson

Many prominent experts in the field of Chiropractic Craniopathy postulate that cranial distortion may have significant if not devastating effects upon brain function. After all, notable differences can be found between the right and left sides of the head, as related to the Category II pelvic distortion pattern.

When the sutures subluxate in the DCS, the head bones distort in a three-dimensional manner. This can mean one side of the head is pressing more firmly into the brain cavity, while the other is not, as illustrated in the MRI below of a human brain. The effect of the skull's pressure results in one side of the brain appearing compressed. It's theorized that the compressed side may not function as well as it should, since as little as one ounce of pressure can alter brain nerve function. At this point, it should be noted that despite the asymmetrical nature of the brain in this MRI, it is considered "normal."

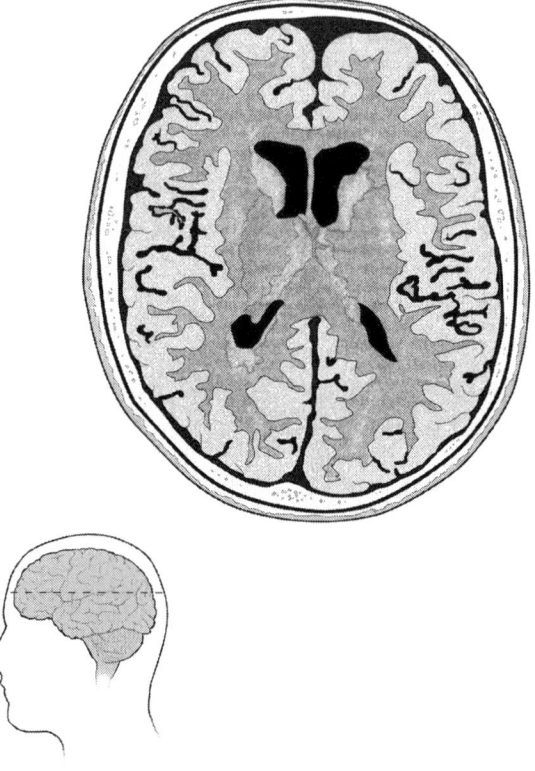

Figure 21: *In this reproduction of an actual MRI, it is easy to see that the internal structures of this cranium are not identical right and left. This asymmetry is thought to play a potential role in disturbed neurology, cerebral spinal fluid flow, blood flow and lymphatic drainage. In turn, health can be compromised in a multitude of ways throughout the body.*

Dr. Jonathan Howat of Oxford, England is one of the prominent experts championing this compressed brain theory. His section 2 of his classic text, *Chiropractic*, there are a series of additional MRIs that illustrate brain distortions considered medically normal. It also thoroughly examines the CSRM. The book is intended for chiropractic physicians; however, it is invaluable for anyone interested in gaining a greater understanding of cranial distortion and CSRM.

Physical Responses to Cranial Distortion

The brain is exquisitely sensitive and must coordinate millions of nerve firings every second to maintain normal function. This is a huge job and must be coordinated perfectly. When pressure is present, it alters nerve-firing patterns. Therefore, any additional pressures inside the head could easily distort and interfere with nerve transmissions. It's easy to see how cranial subluxations may be crucial to brain function and involved with many diseases and conditions.

Even when brain asymmetry is present, the MRI is considered medically normal because it's so commonplace to see these distortions. Experts consider these distortions unremarkable since, in most cases, those with the distortion don't appear to be suffering.

However, this is not the whole story. Different people react differently to all sorts of things. For example, pollen is a very tiny, almost microscopic substance that does not affect everyone in the same way. Does that mean that it's insignificant? Of course not! One individual may have full-blown reactions to the pollen while another person may have none. Similarly, cranial subluxations may affect some people more so than others.

Certain clinical evidence supports these theories. The positive, sometimes life-changing responses of patients to Chiropractic Craniopathy treatments have been most encouraging. Which compels the question: Why then does Chiropractic Craniopathy not enjoy the recognition it deserves?

The reasons are complex. For one, the scientific community primarily relies upon controlled double-blind studies. This type of research attempts to control every possible variable. A sizable group of individuals with any single condition or symptom is given the exact same treatment over time. Another group with the same condition or symptom is given a fake treatment or placebo. At the conclusion of the study, the data is analyzed to determine if and by how much change occurred. This type of study works well for pharmaceutical drug testing, but less well for treatments that can produce unpredictable results, as in Chiropractic Craniopathy.

For example, consider the headache. One strategy for treating headaches is to administer a pain medication that effectively interferes with the pain. A person suffering from the headaches still has the conditions that caused the headache; however, they don't feel the pain due to the pain reliever.

An alternative approach would be to determine and attempt to resolve the cause of the headaches. Many headache sufferers have reported a variety of effective measures ranging from rest to psychological counseling, a vitamin or nutrient, or a series of cranial adjustments to resolve their headaches. Often other treatments had failed, but each person found a treatment that yielded positive results unique to that person. There isn't a single fix for most conditions, even if the symptoms are identical.

Therefore, if we took a large group of individuals suffering from headaches and gave them a specific cranial adjustment or performed the complete sutural procedures, we would probably not see good results because the procedure given may not be what they need to stop their headache. The failure of this type of research is usually not a fault of the intervention but the unique makeup of the patient.

Nutritional Deficiencies

Sometimes physical responses are rooted in nutritional deficiencies. For example, a person suffering from tension headaches gets them because she has too much muscular tension in her upper body that's causing additional and abnormal stresses upon the cranium. The constant muscle tension pulls down on the head and causes pain in the form of headaches.

It is essential to note that muscles do not have any independent function of their own. A muscle alone is incapable of action. The nerve supply to the muscle directs all its actions. Only when the muscle has a nerve telling it to do so, will it contract. Therefore, the muscle tension can only be caused by some nerve irritation.

My role as a clinician is to observe and identify the root cause of the pain, not simply mask the symptom. In this case, I would wonder what could be causing the nerve irritation. There are many possibilities, but a logical conclusion is a calcium deficiency because adequate calcium levels are required for nerve relaxation. If the nerves can't relax, the muscle becomes tight and tense.

Other symptoms accompanying this deficiency include muscle cramps that are often worse at night and headaches, especially upon waking. A lack of adequate calcium may also cause restless leg syndrome, insomnia and fatigue from a lack of quality sleep. The undue tensions could also be produced by a magnesium deficiency, spinal subluxation, reaction to a prescribed medication or any number of other possibilities, including cranial subluxations.

The simple fact is that any symptom may have a variety of causes. The proper solution must be applied to guarantee successful results. A nutritional supplement will not correct a cranial subluxation and cranial treatment cannot resolve a nutritional deficiency.

The key to finding a solution is giving the person what she needs to correct the problem. The same solution doesn't work for every person, even if the problem seems identical. Therefore, classic double-blind clinical trials may not demonstrate effectiveness, even if the treatment would be of great value to many people.

Of the many patients I have treated, Amy's case illustrates how cranial distortion can affect the whole body in unpredictable ways.

Case Study – Amy

As a paramedic, Amy's vocation aligned perfectly with her life's calling: to help others in great distress, including saving their lives. On a fateful day in 2008, her life changed course dramatically en route to a tragic accident. She was driving the ambulance when an oncoming vehicle suddenly appeared in her lane of traffic. Her instinct was to veer to the side at the last moment to spare her partner the brunt of the impact. The unavoidable head-on collision was concentrated on the driver's side, followed by several additional impacts. Amy was unconscious for most of them.

When she regained consciousness, her first instinct was to perform her job. She attended to the injuries of the irresponsible driver. Once she knew the driver was not in critical danger she submitted to her own evaluation and treatment. Still in shock from the experience, she had no appreciation of the nature and extent of her injuries...yet.

Amy sought my evaluation and treatment three and a half years after the trauma. During that time, severe vertigo had been a constant companion, which she described as feeling as if she was constantly carsick. All treatment and analysis up to that point had failed to diagnosis the cause of her debilitating condition.

Severe, often incapacitating, headaches became the daily norm. She also experienced other head pains, neck pain, low back and hip pains, along with difficulties with digestion, severe fatigue and shoulder pain. To make matters even worse, there were unpredictable episodes of vision loss in her right eye, which were accompanied by burning head pains, as well as aggravated neck and shoulder symptoms.

While some of the symptoms were intermittent and varied in intensity, the nausea and stomach issues were a constant problem. Initially, she could only eat a tiny bit and had great difficulty keeping almost anything down. She quickly lost a considerable amount of weight pushing her toward anorexia. Recognizing the obvious danger of inadequate nutrition, she forced herself to eat what she could, praying it would stay down. She already had enough problems without adding things such as muscular wasting, fatigue, depression or other symptoms of malnutrition to her list. None of the extensive medical testing she submitted to could determine the cause for her multiple, severe symptoms. Medically, there was nothing wrong with her.

Amy's job depended upon her being in exceptional physical condition. She forced herself to walk six to seven miles daily. As time passed, new problems cropped up. Despite being barely able to eat anything and continuing her exercise program, she mysteriously gained 40 pounds. Something was terribly wrong. Her biochemistry had gone awry. Her physical condition presented a most perplexing situation. Physiologically, an organism can't expend energy while not taking in sufficient calories and still gain weight. Her attending physicians thought she was crazy, and Amy was inclined to agree.

Yet, all her symptoms are classic manifestations from closed head injuries, even the weight gain. It all goes back to cranial distortion. The pituitary gland, considered the master gland of the body, is located in the center of the cranium's bony structures. Disturbances and distortions in cranial function can affect the function of the pituitary gland by either depressing it or stimulating it. Because the pituitary affects almost every hormone-producing gland in the body, the effects from a disturbance can be unpredictable, diverse and contradictory.

The medical evaluations following Amy's injuries revealed some minor issues in the cervical and lumbar spines. Other than that, nothing was found to be medically wrong with her. She even saw a neuropsychiatrist. *In the first minute of the first session, this medical doctor announced that all her problems were due to childhood sexual abuse. The diagnosis was curious given that he had just met her. More curious, neither she, nor her siblings had any recollection of ever experiencing abuse.*

It's likely this determination was made, in part, because the other medical tests were normal. In the absence of concrete indications of serious dysfunction or pathology, it's possible this physician was attempting to look deeper to uncover the potential cause of her condition. The power of the subconscious mind is formidable, and anything is possible. If Amy was suffering from the effects of such a deep and disturbing psychological imbalance, then the only intervention that would most likely be of value would be extensive psychoanalysis and/ or psychotherapy.

The whole situation seemed horrific and desperate to Amy, and her entire family was concerned. In this age of modern medicine, technology and resources, they couldn't fathom why no reasons for Amy's condition had been found. Amy was beginning to feel as if there were nowhere to turn.

Financial pressures mounted. Because her injuries prevented her from doing her job, and since a psychiatrist diagnosed her with a pre-existing psychological problem, Amy was fired. This meant she had no health insurance. She also couldn't obtain legal satisfaction from the young driver who caused the accident, as he was uninsured. She had obtained treatment through Workers' Compensation, but it ended with the psychiatrist's diagnosis.

This would have crushed a lesser person. Amy firmly believed she could recover from this crisis. Her husband and family were support-

ive, but everyone else told her she was making it up, crazy or out to gain financially. It seemed that no one would believe her, and no one could help her. She did experience temporary relief from her local chiropractic physician who could reduce the severity of her symptoms when the extreme flare-ups occurred. This caring doctor was able to relieve her symptoms but was not successful at getting the problems to resolve permanently.

Amy remained dedicated to her ultimate goal, which was to be of greater service to humankind. It seemed as if the sheer force of her will and intent worked in some mysterious fashion to bring about our first meeting. Amy lives many, many hundreds of miles away. As it turns out, her father lives in my hometown.

Amy's father is health conscious and has received the benefits of Samantha, a brilliant cranial sacral therapist, who lives and practices in my neighborhood. Dad related his daughter's condition to her and wondered if she could help Amy, who was going to be in town for a short visit. For some mysterious or simply intuitive reason, Samantha thought of me. She was not at all familiar with the Category II cranial sutural dysfunction (DCS) or of SOT. She just had a hunch.

Luckily, I had time to visit Amy at Samantha's office. My initial examination revealed a severe Category II subluxation complex, including extreme fixation of the cranial sutural system. She presented with a clear and serious case of DCS.

I explained how the Category II system works and why it's important in the body. I proposed performing a full ISP. This was a tremendous amount of therapeutic input for a first treatment, but time was short, as she was returning home the next day. I wanted to know if the DCS could be the root of her problems and if the full cranial sutural proce-

dure could help her. We agreed that if the treatment helped, she would then make whatever arrangements necessary to restore her health, no matter what it took.

I explained that the effectiveness of the treatment would be enhanced by identifying and focusing on her goals. When I asked Amy what was most important to her, she said, "to have my memory back." Prior to the accident, she had a near photographic memory; now she was having difficulty with any short-term information. Her reason was simple. She was working toward certification as an emergency medical technician with the intent of becoming a physician's assistant one day. She wanted to help people, and this is how she planned to do it. Despite all the pain and suffering she was experiencing, what was most important to her was to have her mind and memory back so she could continue her life's calling to help others.

I was honored to assist a person so fiercely devoted to helping others, Now I also had a mission. Number one was to assist Amy in achieving her vision for her future. Number two was to remove as much stress and tension from the cranial sutural system as was possible–with this one treatment. By relieving these stresses, her brain and nervous system could function better. Maybe some of the pains and tension would diminish, but more importantly, her brain and memory could work better.

Amy exhibited extreme fixations in multiple areas of her cranium, and we engaged in a lengthy session of corrections. We made significant clinical progress, and an hour later Amy stood up without vomiting. Prior to this treatment, any repositioning from lying to standing usually made her feel nauseated. She also noted the vertigo was completely gone for the first time since the accident. Three and a half years of constant dizziness and nausea were instantly gone, at least for now.

She was physically steadier. She could stand straighter without wobbling versus how she presented when I examined her an hour earlier. Her overall levels of pain had diminished considerably. The headache that was evident at the beginning of the treatment was completely gone. We slowly made our way to the reception area where Amy's dad and Samantha were anxiously waiting. They both remarked as to how different Amy looked. The old Amy had reemerged.

After the treatment, Amy's brain began functioning differently. It was sending clear signals, which resulted in a significant reduction in the tension in her shoulders, neck and head. Her low back pain wasn't completely gone but it felt considerably better. I explained to her dad and Samantha what we had found and what I had done.

As I talked, Amy kept looking out the window across the street and covering one eye and then the other. Her vision had been fuzzy and not working well ever since the accident. She suddenly exclaimed, "Oh my God!" She continued covering each eye and looking wildly about, first at something close to her in the room and then across the room. Then she would look outside and then back into the room. Fearful that something may have gone wrong, her dad rushed to her side.

Amy stopped her frenetic movements, and a big smile lit up her face. She explained that she could see color through both eyes again. She hadn't realized until that moment that her color vision had been gone in her right eye since the injury. Her eyes were focusing as they should, and her color perception had returned as well. Amy was truly a happy camper.

She always believed that she could recover from her injuries. Now the possibilities of such a recovery were made real to her in a short time.

She cried but not too much. She had better things to do, like starting to plan for her next training and classes.

As would be expected, her symptoms are not 100 percent gone, and they do fluctuate. At her last evaluation, she estimated that her overall symptom levels were approximately 50 percent of what they were prior to our first full cranial sutural treatment. She has also rated herself 80 percent asymptomatic at times.

Based on her positive results from the first treatment, it was clear that Amy's problems were trauma-induced from the accident. The cranial sutural system was conclusively involved, and we would have to address other cranial and spinal issues in her ongoing treatment. These cases are often a bit slow in recovery, and the physician must evaluate each step that is needed and adjust the treatment plan when progress plateaus. To date, Amy has made amazing improvements given the nature and extent of her injuries and the minimal interventions that had been provided before. In this way, she is uncharacteristic in her response.

In other words, her recovery is occurring far faster than is typical. I can never completely explain why some people respond faster than others do. I suspect that her determination plays an important role in her healing. Amy has lofty goals and intentions. Our minds, spirits and bodies are said to take inspiration from our higher intent. Amy's body is doing all that it can to achieve her goals. This may sound a bit unscientific, and it is. However, there are many real-life examples to consider that substantiate this belief.

Stephen Hawking hasn't let his ailing body deter him from his amazing contributions to science. Milton Erickson, MD accomplished great things while suffering from several forms of multiple sclerosis. We all know of people or have family members who have endured great hardships in service to others. Focused will and powerful intentions are great allies. Still, there are times when will and intention alone are not enough to get the job done. We need the support of a properly functioning physical system, especially the brain and spinal cord.

While the initial results of treatment have been impressive if not miraculous, Amy clearly has a long way to go. From my experience, she will be dealing with the results of these injuries for quite some time. It is unknown if her condition is permanent. She may never fully recover to the state of health she enjoyed prior to the accident. What is known is that she will require–and receive–consistent intervention from fully-trained professionals certified in these advanced procedures. Given Amy's dedication and her unshakable faith, I have no doubt she will ultimately overcome and live the life she desires helping others.

My vision is that an understanding of how the structural systems influence the mental, emotional and physical functioning of a human being will bring about wider acceptance. Then maybe more people would seek proper treatment and more physicians would be inspired to dedicate themselves to the additional effort and hard work required to become proficient at delivering this kind of service to humanity. Additionally, perhaps wider interest would generate more research funding to the Sacro Occipital Research Society, Inc. (SORSI) for essential studies to further understand the role of Craniopathy in head trauma, degenerative brain diseases and general health.

Chapter 6

Category II Self-Test

When you know the truth, the truth makes you a soldier.
– Gandhi

As previously noted, Chiropractic Craniopathy is the philosophy, art and science of treating the cranium, structurally and functionally, as performed by chiropractic physicians. Cranial therapies have proven to be quite beneficial, and even produce miraculous results. This book is dedicated to more fully informing and expanding understanding of Chiropractic Craniopathy and associated complex cranial treatment methods that have been overlooked and underappreciated.

Who needs Chiropractic Craniopathy?

Anyone can benefit from Chiropractic Craniopathy, especially as other treatments fail to achieve results. Chiropractic Craniopathy is especially beneficial for those suffering from a brain injury or degenerative brain condition, including Multiple Sclerosis, Alzheimer's, Parkinson's, Traumatic Brain Injury (TBI), and concussions. Chiropractic Craniopathy treatments should be a part of any comprehensive brain healing program, along with exercise, diet and nutrition, and can be further applied to the treatment protocol for heavy metal toxicity, gut healing, autoimmune disorders, and genetic health issues.

Chiropractic Craniopathy is particularly beneficial for those who suffer from the De Jarnette Cranial Syndrome (DCS) involving the pelvis, spine and cranium. The cranial sacral respiratory mechanism (CSRM) - the structures and mechanisms of the body producing and distributing cerebral spinal fluid (CSF) - is an essential part of how the brain heals the whole body. The Integrated Sutural Protocols (ISP) address the human cranium in ways unlike all other cranial therapies. If cranial subluxations are the source of health issues, no other intervention will work quite the same.

When a disturbance exists in the CSRM, a profound neurological compromise occurs, producing effects; specifically, the portion of the brain that is responsible for evaluating your exact position in time and space (scientifically called proprioception) is disturbed.

The following self-test can be done at home to see if there is any suggestion of Category II dysfunction and/or cranial sutural restrictions or jamming. The **only way to know for sure** is to be evaluated by a Certified Craniopath. The test is based on the neurological effects of a disturbance in the Category II portion of the Craniosacral Respiratory Mechanism (CSRM).

At Home Test

Begin the test by positioning yourself near a wall or stable object. This way, if you become unstable during the test, you can reach for something to steady your body.

If you find yourself particularly unstable at any time, terminate this test immediately. In some individuals, standing as instructed can produce extreme instability, and may be an indication of a significant problem in the Category II and related sutural mechanism.

- Stand up with your feet together and touching, looking straight ahead.

  If your feet can't touch, the test may not be valid. A Category II dysfunction diagnosis will require a certified SOT practitioner.

- While standing still with your arms at your sides, close your eyes and try to remain perfectly still. Do you find yourself becoming more unstable?

  The normal person without any Category II dysfunction might move very slightly from side to side. This motion is no greater than one fourth of an inch, which is imperceptible to most individuals. If you find yourself moving side to side or front to back, it could suggest a Category II dysfunction. This is because your brain cannot quite precisely tell where it is in time and space (proprioception). What you are feeling is your brain telling your muscle system to search for your center of gravity.

- Continue standing. Close your eyes again. If it's safe for you, take in a full deep breath and hold it. Does your motion change for better or worse?

- Next, force your breath entirely out and hold it, again noting changes or differences in your body's motion.

- Finally, still standing with feet together, arms at your sides and looking straight ahead, place a pencil, tongue depressor, popsicle stick or anything that is relatively thin on the right side of your mouth. You'll be testing how biting something on that side affects your balance. Don't bite hard. Note if this affects your overall balance and stability. Now take the object and place it in the other side of your mouth, holding it as you did before. Note any differences in your overall stability.

While these tests are suggestive only, if any of these experiments produced either significant instability in your structure or if they increased instability, then you may want to see a Certified Craniopath for a Category II Subluxation analysis.

Please note: if you don't move at all, it can be an indication of a different problem outside the scope of this book. Dr. De Jarnette described this as a Category III dysfunction.

Chapter 7
Cranial Adjustments and the Mind

"Be proud of what you think you know only after you fully appreciate how much you do not understand. You do not need to know how healing works but you must know that you can heal."

– Albert Einstein

Sages through the ages have attempted to impress upon us the true power of the human mind. What we think and how we perceive the world can have a great influence on our ability to manifest goals and dreams in life. How and what we think plays a huge role in what we achieve and experience. Even more important are our unconscious goals and thoughts. That is the part of the manifestation processes of which we are unaware yet affects us more than we can imagine.

Imagine the potential if we could gather up and harness our subconscious processes! What kind of power could we manifest if we could consciously focus and direct the energies of the unconscious mind? Even more exciting, what if this power could be enhanced or amplified beyond its normal limits? The outcomes would be unpredictable, surprising and delightful.

Dr. De Jarnette always emphasized the importance of focus and will. When performing cranial procedures, he felt it was essential to have the entire focus on not only what is being done on the patient, but also the desired outcome. The added measures of focused intent and directed will provide an invaluable dimension to the healing process.

With respect to the full sutural procedure (ISP), he would repeatedly insist that the doctor and patient must think of absolutely nothing but the desired goal. Furthermore, it was imperative that, as much as possible, no other stray thoughts be allowed to enter the mind. The doctor was repeatedly told to keep his personal thoughts to himself and focus upon his healing task only. These key ingredients allow the sutural process to produce results far beyond the expectations of the simple mechanical process of relieving head tensions and facilitating CSF pressure reduction and flow.

Optimal brain function, in all its manifestations, is enhanced by the sutural procedure and affords a powerful surge of vital energy to the brain and mind. By giving these mysterious subconscious processes precise direction and focus, we greatly increase the chances of realizing our goals.

How can this possibly work? It turns out that the innate vitality that fuels physical healing also energizes the entire mental, emotional and physical gestalt (the total) of the person. By focusing, a person's will or intent defines a specific goal or outcome giving direction to the innate vital force. In other words, we can focus our energy toward specific outcomes, not unlike a laser can focus light on a specific target. The same amount of energy can illuminate a room but it's less specific.

The cranium and sutural systems are essential in the production and distribution of CSF, which is associated with the innate vital force of the person. If a person, through will and intent, focuses on desires and outcomes, then the person as a whole — mentally, emotionally, physically, consciously and unconsciously — will move toward those goals.

In most cases, when the ISP is implemented, the effect is directed toward relieving a physical discomfort. Therefore, some positive change of the physical symptoms can be seen. At times, however, no matter how debilitating the physical pain may be, the person receiving a full sutural treatment may not experience any reduction in her symptoms or conditions. Instead, she may have to hunt for changes that occur somewhere else in her being. Often, an emotional shift ends up facilitating the physical healing process.

Because mental and emotional changes can be wrought through the ISP, some people have utilized the full cranial sutural technique to enhance their skills in creative pursuits. Others have used it to overcome specific problems, such as fears or phobias, or to help facilitate changing unwanted personal habits. Others have used the procedure to help achieve business or personal goals.

This is a valuable and intriguing use of the ISP, in which situations may or may not involve specific physical symptoms or conditions. In other words, the person may be perfectly healthy, or the individual may have health concerns at the same time as working on specific intentions beyond the physical.

John Grinder, PhD truly understands and emphasizes the role of neurology on our behavior. His work focuses on understand the interrelationship between the mental, emotional and physical aspects of human functioning. One major premise is that if any mental, emotional or physical function of the human can be brought to its highest level of potential, then all other components will also upgrade accordingly.

I worked with a talented Ironman triathlon athlete. These extreme athletes swim 2.4 miles then sprint to their bicycles and engage in a heated bicycle race 112 miles long. They then run a marathon, which is 26.2 miles. The fastest triathletes in the world accomplish all this work in approximately 8 hours. This athlete had been competing in Ironman triathlons and training for several years. He was very good at it. He came to me because he wanted to do even better. I analyzed his Category II complex and found that it was not perfectly aligned, and he also had cranial sutural fixations. We worked together over approximately three months to realign the Category II system and resolve some of his cranial sutural fixations. He trimmed about 45 minutes off his average triathlon.

It could be that alleviating his Category II distortion and cranial sutural issues had nothing to do with his performance, but he believed it did.

The effects of a properly treated Category II complex and sutural system can increase and balance neuromuscular coordination. It can also enhance vitality and overall function. While these effects are not proven by any scientific research studies, they have been widely experienced by practitioners and their clients worldwide for many decades.

For example, if a person enters any activity with full and complete expectation (mental attitude) of delivering his absolute best performance, the outcome will be vastly different than if he performs the same activity (physical), with a full expectation of failure. If a person is running the 100-yard dash expecting to do poorly, the physical performance will likely be diminished. If the same person embraces a winning attitude, the physical effort will probably be markedly improved.

A colleague, Dr. Darryl Oblack, related an impressive example of the use of the ISP for goal manifestation. One of his patients, a hardworking and talented artist, came to him with a dilemma. She was a skilled businessperson who worked hard to attract agents, locate exhibit opportunities and identify other avenues to showcase her creative and unique works of art. Nothing was working. Her art wasn't selling.

Dr. Oblack and the artist focused on the desired outcome of selling her art. They didn't try to figure out how this should happen by envisioning the steps that needed to occur. Instead, they held the images of the outcome, sales of artwork, in their minds as the doctor performed a full cranial sutural procedure. Their focus and directed intent must have worked, as her next month sales more than quadrupled. That's not bad for a one-hour intervention. The results could be passed off as improvements in her marketing or other unknown circumstances. However, over the following months the results continued.

All of this could be purely coincidental, although the artist was convinced the ISP had had an effect. The uptick in sales while undergoing the ISP interventions for goal setting were, to her, clearly unlike anything she had previously experienced.

Sutural procedures or Chiropractic Craniopathy at large is not a cure for all things. While this process had ongoing benefits for the artist for an impressive period, they didn't continue indefinitely. Eventually, her sales slumped. The artist thought that Dr. Oblack had stopped performing the procedure correctly. For his part, Dr. Oblack wondered if his patient had missed something in his technique.

Obviously, nothing cures everything all the time for everyone. These procedures tap into the mysterious and poorly understood inner mechanisms of human function. Many times, this potential can be unleashed by the proper cranial procedure; however, it's not the complete answer. Still, we should never underestimate the miraculous potential of a human being and the ability of the individual to heal from all types of problems—mental, emotional and physical—when given the proper avenues to do so.

Chapter 8

Measuring Change

*"There were never so many able, active minds at work
on the problems of diseases as now, and all of their
discoveries are attending to the simple truth — that you
cannot improve upon nature."*

– Thomas A. Edison

The full potential of identifying and correcting cranial bone subluxations
has yet to be discovered. Critical investigative research is needed to refine
diagnostic measures to predict the needs of any given patient and even
identify when these therapies are required. This chapter explores some of
the possibilities.

Lasca Hospers PhD, DC was working with a patient who presented
abnormal results from a brain mapping study. Upon examination of the
patient, it was discovered that the Category II subluxation complex was
present. Dr. Hospers only corrected the pelvic torque. After one hour,
the patient submitted to another EEG. The results of the retest showed
significant improvement in brain function. With enough funding, more
of these studies could be performed.

Advancements in brain imaging include new MRI technology that
can capture CSF flow. This type of tool would be helpful when analyzing
people suffering from the DCS. With enough study, it may be possible
to identify this condition using new MRI methods. Furthermore, results
could be measured following treatment to evaluate changes in CSF flow.

Facial recognition software offers intriguing possibilities for Chiropractic Craniopathy research. Using state-of-the-art programs that
provide a sophisticated means for analyzing facial features, researchers

could measure minute craniofacial changes due to pelvic alignment. This type of research could prove most beneficial in identifying and treating certain cranial subluxations.

Several of the patients highlighted in this book suffered from moderate to severe closed head injuries. These traumas cause billions of dollars of mental, emotional, physical and financial damages. Clinical research could not only trim these costs but also save lives.

Kineseology Testing Research

Some of the performance changes I have witnessed in patients are intriguing. Research in the Category II subluxation complex and its mechanisms, as well as DCS, is sorely needed. One important ingredient in any research study involves the ability to measure change in test subjects.

Chiropractic physicians can sometimes have profound effects on a person but not be able to objectively or accurately measure those effects at the time of the intervention or treatment. Knowing this has always intrigued me with respect to the Category II and cranial sutural treatments. Because we know that the Category II system, when compromised, negatively affects the body's ability to determine its position in time and space, I postulated the theory that this effect could be demonstrated through kinesiology or muscle strength testing.

Kinesiology was originally a medical testing procedure used to evaluate the strength of various muscles in the body. Muscles themselves are brainless. They're connected to the brain by nerves, which tell the muscle what to do. The nerve doesn't act independently; it receives signals from the brain or other reflexes. Therefore, if a person is holding her arm up and the doctor pushes on the patient's hand, as illustrated below, the anterior deltoid muscle is being specifically tested. The brain tells the nerve to tell the muscle to hold strong as the doctor pushes on the arm to evaluate the nerve integrity and the resulting muscle strength.

It stands to reason that if the brain's ability to perceive the exact position of the arm is compromised, it will have less available focus and strength than it would if the neuromuscular system was functioning properly. In other words, if there is some interruption of the nerve signal to the muscle being tested, it would be weak when it should be strong. It is important to note that the nerve and muscle here work as a unit directed by the brain. I decided to conduct a study to assess whether an individual with a significantly compromised Category II system, can or cannot manifest his full complement of strength when he undergoes kinesiological testing.

To conduct my study, I selected a group of patients who all had indicators of an active Category II subluxation complex and cranial sutural dysfunction. I tested 16 muscles on each individual before and after treatment. Each of those muscles was tested with a hand-held dynamometer.

A dynamometer is a device that measures pressure. I used this device to push on a specific part of each appendage (arm or leg) involved and pushed hard enough to overcome that muscle's strength. In other words, I was measuring the hardest the muscle could push back on the dynamometer.

Each person had the following muscles tested for strength. These tests were done on both sides of the body (bilaterally).

Pectoralis major sterna	Psoas
Pectoralis major clavicular	Tensor fascia lata
Anterior deltoid	Adductors
Latissimus dorsi	Gluteus medius

For this study, the participant did not stand or leave the table until he or she went through repeat testing following the treatment. The pelvic twist associated with the Category II subluxation complex was corrected using SOT orthopedic wedges, as designed and engineered by Dr. De Jarnette. Also, the entire Category II treatment protocol was performed. This protocol is required to completely un-torque both the cranial (head) and pelvic (hips) ends of the Category II and the cranial sutural systems. The results were significant. Within recognized scientific parameters, muscle strength improved in all individuals following the correction of their Category II sacroiliac subluxation and basic sutural distortions. (Refer to Appendix B for the study Abstract.)

Craniofacial Dynamics and the Pelvis

DCS places a different type of stress pattern into the cranium than is typically described throughout the rest of Craniopathy. If you have previous training in Chiropractic Craniopathy or Craniosacral Therapy (CST), some of the descriptions in this book may not seem logical to you. There are several related, but distinctly different, mechanisms at work in the body. They produce forces into the cranium resulting in a variety of possible distortion patterns. The DCS pattern is different from the movement patterns that are traditionally described in other theories of cranial function.

If you are one of these advanced students, try to understand that the motions typically attributed to the CSRM are still functional and continue to operate within the distortion patterns described by the DCS.

There are at least two major influences upon cranial motion. One is the traditional CSRM, which was first described by early investigators in Craniopathy. Osteopathic and chiropractic research has measured the motions to be in the vicinity of ten thousandths of an inch. The second is the cranial sutural system. There is a rhythmical expansion and contraction of this mechanism. No matter how tiny, it is of great importance to the physiological function of the brain and ultimately the control mechanisms of the entire brain and nervous system. In turn, the nervous system controls or influences almost every other aspect of the body.

DCS involves the second and different but related mechanism. The DCS is more mechanical and doesn't undergo the rhythmical expansion and contraction as we see in the CSRM. Both are at work at the same time. In other words, the DCS can cause significant distortion in the cranium and at the same time, the CSRM is still producing its tiny expansions and contractions. These two mechanisms are intimately interwoven.

The effects of DCS upon the cranium are mechanically much larger in magnitude than that of the CSRM. The amount of motion involved can often be seen with the naked eye. This is not true for the CSRM. Normal CSRM motion can be felt by a trained practitioner and is an important function that needs to be balanced. However, you cannot see this motion by simply watching it. Cranial changes due to the DCS have been measured at up to several millimeters (about 1/16th to 1/32nd of an inch) rather than in ten thousandths of an inch. This is an amount of motion that, in some individuals, can be seen by visual observation.

We are describing two different mechanisms. Both are essential for the health of the whole body. Both mechanisms are important. Therapeutically, the more important one is that which the patient is having the most problem with at a given time. They both affect each other. Both are also essential for normal neurological and physiological functions. Each of these systems, however, must be treated differently.

When I began observing the phenomenon of the significant cranial changes with respect to pelvic corrections, I was skeptical. However, after witnessing virtually instantaneous changes hundreds of times, I decided to conduct a research project at Logan University.

A photographic camera was suspended in a stationary position pointing down toward the face of the subject. Perpendicular and parallel markers were placed on either side of the head and held tightly up against the temporal bones, the most lateral sides of the head. A line was also drawn exactly in the center of the bridge of the nose.

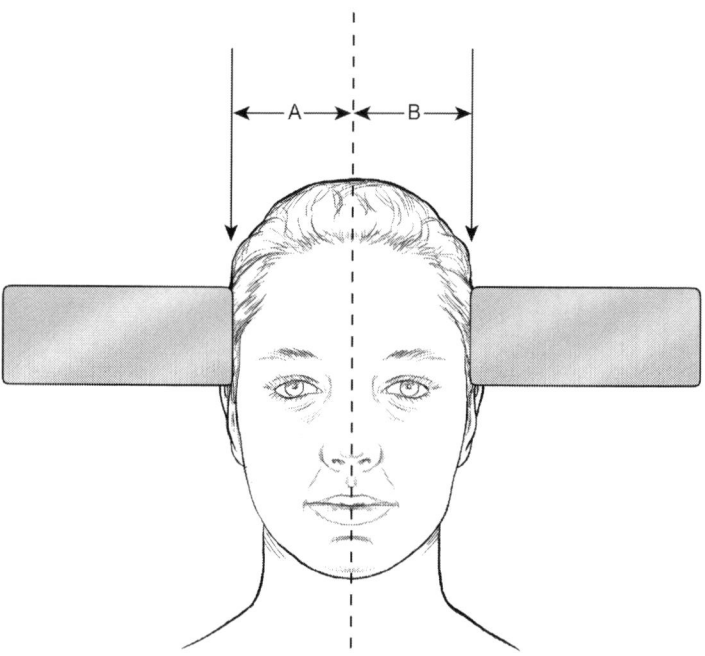

Figure 22: *To evaluate possible changes in the cranium, markers were used as illustrated and were perpendicular to a stationary flat surface. The distances from the center of the head to the sides of the temporal bones were measured on each side, with and without the Category II blocks.*

A picture was taken while the subject remained on the table. Without analyzing if or what direction the subject's pelvis might be twisted, levers were placed under the hips designed to untwist the crooked pelvis. In the DCS there are two possibilities. In one situation, the left hip rotates backwards, and the right hip moves forward. In the other possibility, the opposite occurs: the left hip rotates forward and the right hip moves backwards.

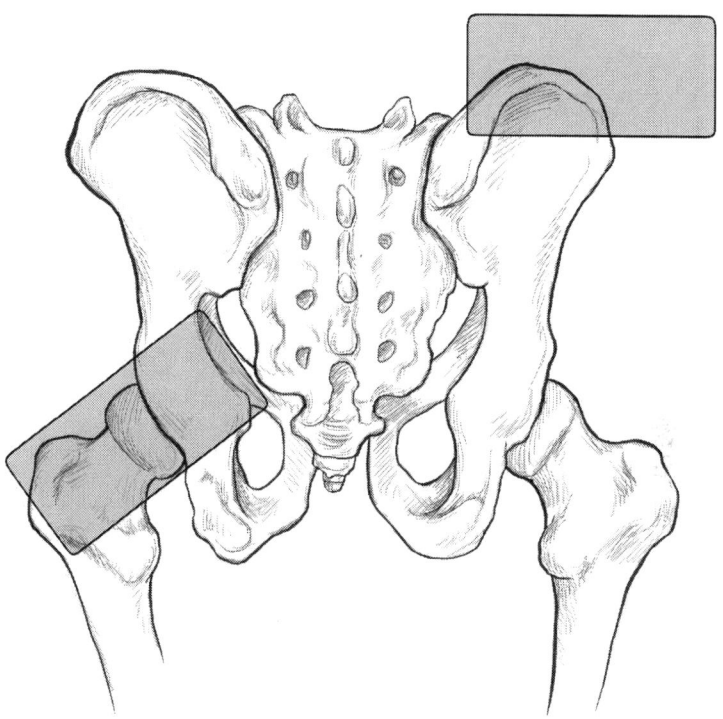

Figure 23: *Dr. De Jarnette, along with research from independent engineers, developed orthopedic wedges designed to precisely counteract the pelvic torsion found in the Category II subluxation complex as well as other pelvic and lumbar subluxations. The research project evaluating the relationship between the pelvic torsion and cranial subluxations used his mechanical wedges as illustrated.*

It should be noted that this particular distortion, the Category II subluxation complex and the accompanying DCS, are sensitive to proper treatment. If the procedures are performed improperly, the results will not be optimal. I have seen many patients that have experienced increased pain levels from improper treatment procedures of this nature. Therefore, a certified SOT chiropractic physician is the only choice for proper diagnosis and treatment.

In the Logan research project, the pelvis was next blocked for the left posterior (subluxated toward the back) and right anterior (subluxated toward the front) pelvic distortion complex. After about 30 seconds, another photo was taken of the head. As noted above, the patient remained stationary throughout this entire process and did not move off the table.

The blocks were then reversed as if they were treating the opposite pelvic distortion. Another 30 seconds went by and the third photograph was then taken.

All photographs were taken from the same distance from the participant, and the camera was not moved between any of the images. In this way, a perfect representation of the cranium and face was captured. If there was no obvious mechanical relationship between the head and the pelvis, the photographs would look identical. If DCS represents a plausible theory, then measurable changes may be seen.

Each of the photographs was printed on full sheets of paper approximating the size of each person's head and face. This large pile of photographs was then placed in a random order. The distances between the parallel markers on the sides of the head and the line in the center of the nose were then measured on both the left and right sides. An independent examiner recorded those measurements.

The measurement information was then correlated. What we found reinforced what many practitioners have seen for years. The head changed measurably with respect to distortion of the pelvis.

Of course, there could have been errors in our marking and measuring. Therefore, a second phase of this project was conducted. Another group of subjects was recruited and went through the entire photographic process as described above. There was one exception. None of these patients had blocks under their pelvis for any of the photos. If there were no errors in our measuring process, then all the markings and measurements on the patients who weren't orthopedically blocked would be identical.

Each of the subjects had three photographs taken. As before, each was printed full-size and marked and measured exactly as the previous test subjects. There was indeed a small amount of error identified. However, the error was significantly smaller than the measurements found in the individuals who received the orthopedic blocking.

The findings of this study were found to be scientifically significant by standard statistical analysis. However, one study does not provide conclusive proof. Much more research is needed. (Refer to Appendix C for the study abstract)

Split Face Technique

The amount of change in the human cranium with respect to DCS can vary greatly from individual to individual. It seems to affect some people far more than others. Two people experiencing the exact same trauma may have two very different reactions. One person may never experience any noticeable long-range effects. Another, receiving the exact same injuries, may suffer a lifetime of misery and dysfunction. How can we explain these great variations?

People are built differently from one to the next. Insights into this fact are supported by brilliant research that has been conducted by Dr. Dennis Enis at Logan University, in collaboration with the Biomechanics Department at the University of Missouri-Columbia and St. Louis University School of Medicine.

In the study subjects, one finding of interest is the high degree of imbalance in the design of the human pelvis. People tend to be very asymmetrical. In other words, we are not built identically right and left. Since the pelvis is the center of gravity for the body, any pelvic imbalance or asymmetry will tend to cause greater disturbances and distortions as the effects of these forces travel up the spine to the cranium.

Not only are people imbalanced right and left, this imbalance also varies greatly from person to person. This research affords us significant insights concerning the wide variations of responses people exhibit from similar traumas and stresses. We are simply built to be different.

In addition, some people are far more susceptible to injuries, traumas and instabilities than others. While much more research is needed, the analysis of the DCS in individuals may lend insight as to their susceptibility to stresses and traumas, as well as give us insights into optimal treatments for people suffering from injuries resulting in disturbance of the DCS and the Category II subluxation complex.

After conducting the first study using photographic analysis, I began wondering about additional ways to use this technology. Could we see the facial changes before and after a full sutural treatment for a diagnosed DCS? The trained eye of a Certified Craniopath is usually required to see cranial distortions and subluxations. Could photographs capture what might not be obvious to the untrained eye?

To highlight the cranial changes in the Category II complex, a different method was applied to some cases in order to visualize cranial facial changes. The technique is simple. A photograph is taken and then cut into half. A reverse, or mirror image, of each side is then made. These additional images are then spliced together to make a whole face. The result is three pictures of the same individual. One picture is of the face as we all see it. The next is composed of only the left sides of the head put together to look like one face. The third picture is composed of the two right sides of the head pieced together to make one face.

BEFORE

AFTER

Left side
BEFORE

Left side
AFTER

Right side
BEFORE

Right side
AFTER

Figure 24: *These drawings are taken from live photographs that were taken immediately before and after the application of the Integrated Sutural Protocols™ (ISP). In the first illustration, facial changes are apparent. The next two pair of drawings were made using the split image technique, further accentuating the cranial changes for easier viewing.*

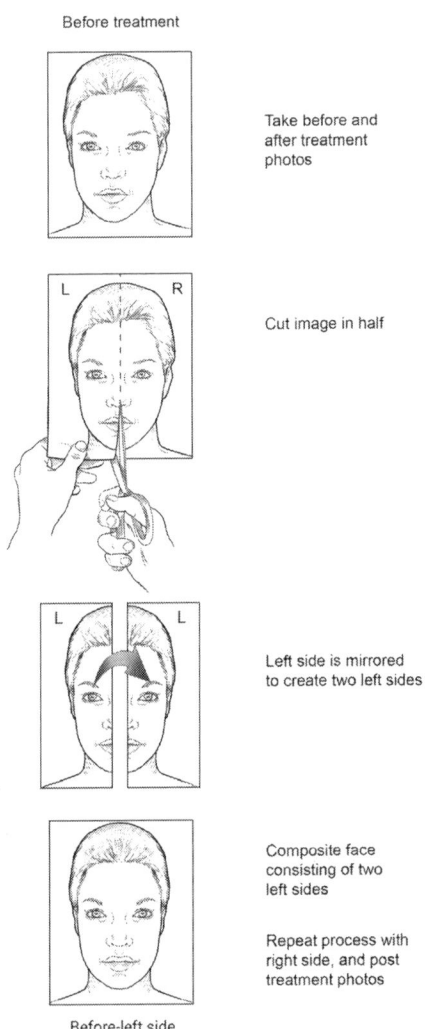

Before treatment

Take before and
after treatment
photos

Cut image in half

Left side is mirrored
to create two left sides

Composite face
consisting of two
left sides

Repeat process with
right side, and post
treatment photos

Before-left side

Figure 25: *Split image technique is used in modern-day cosmetology and plastic surgery to illustrate facial asymmetry. One of the earliest applications was reported by William J Kotheimer, DC, DM in his book "Applied Chiropractic in Distortion Analysis" published in 1976 by Dorrance and Company. Dr. Kotheimer explored these cranial subluxations in relation to imbalances in leg length as produced by subluxations of the human pelvis (hips and sacrum). While the split image technique does not produce an accurate representation of the subject, it assists the untrained eye to visualize the profound differences pre-and post-treatment.*

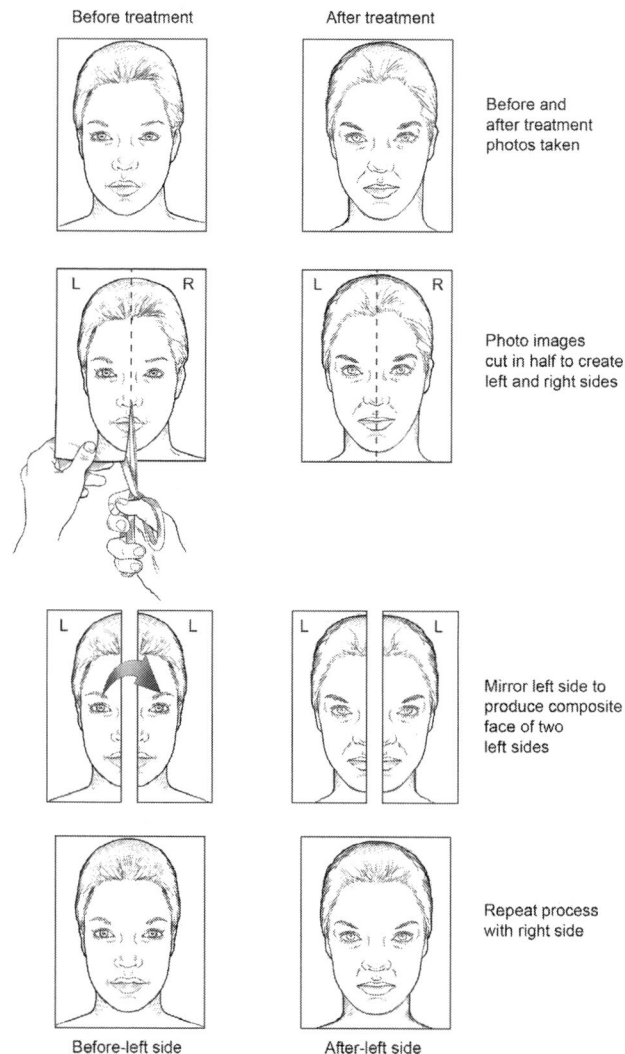

Figure 26: *the detail of the split image process is provided in this set of illustrations.*

This technique shows how unequal or asymmetrical people are in general. Our eye tends to look at a person and automatically correct for these imbalances. We are accustomed to seeing people as they are. The split image procedure accentuates the imbalances. This has become popular enough that several online websites provide a split photo in minutes.

People do not routinely see themselves as they actually appear. When you look in a mirror, which is your most common way of viewing yourself, you are seeing an opposite (mirror) image from what everyone else sees. We are not accustomed to seeing ourselves as other see us.

The first experiment was a somewhat crude and spur of the moment inspiration. I decided to take a photograph just prior to performing a full sutural cranial procedure for DCS. Another photograph was taken immediately following the treatment before the patient got off the table.

This photograph was cut in half and two left sides of the before treatment were spliced together to make one image. Then two halves of the left side were again spliced together from the after-treatment photograph. If no visible changes in the cranium were achieved, then these photographs would look identical. If changes were made, we would see differences from the before and after pictures.

The lighting and angle were a little different between the two photographs, but they still provide insight into the effects of the DCS procedure. The patient is Anthony from an earlier chapter who experienced remarkable improvements in his memory and brain function following the treatment as documented by these photographs. These were taken after Anthony's third full cranial sutural procedure for DCS. The figure presented here is an artist's rendering or those photographs.

The dramatic differences beg the question as to what kind of massive changes in the size and shape of the various internal cranial compartments were made by this treatment. Further, what changes in brain neurology occurred due to the changes made by the full cranial sutural procedure for the DCS?

Figure 27: *Taken from an actual photographic study this illustration depicts another subject immediately before and after application of the Integrated Sutural Protocols™ (ISP). Notice the observable changes in the face and cranial structures resulting in a balancing effect upon intracranial pressures.*

Researchers have discovered that symmetry is one measurable aspect in the perception of beauty. Faces that are more symmetrical are generally perceived to be more attractive than asymmetrical faces. Much of this research is used in the industry of cosmetic surgery where many procedures are designed to produce greater symmetry. One can only hope individuals undergoing these operations don't suffer from DCS that might be corrected at some time following surgeries.

The full cranial procedure often can produce remarkable changes in facial symmetry. If surgery is provided to correct facial asymmetries on a patient that also has a Category II subluxation complex and DCS, the face may appear straighter. If the DCS is then corrected the face will again likely become crooked...in the opposite direction.

Even more important are the neurological changes. All the persons presented in these photographic studies experienced significant changes in brain function, pain reduction and other conditions or complaints. In other words, we often see a direct correlation between the changes produced in the head and the person's mental, emotional and physical condition.

Dr. De Jarnette recommended a series of seven treatments to start. He also insisted that these not be made more than one per month when performing the entire procedure. In between these monthly full cranial sutural treatments, other protocols addressing the Category II subluxation complex are performed weekly, or even more frequently, depending on the patient and the condition.

Factors that may influence the longevity and permanence of these treatments are the nature and extent of injuries and traumas, as well as the genetic build of the specific person in both the pelvis and the cranium. Chronicity (how long the person has had the problem) is another major factor. A recent injury is more likely to respond more quickly than one 30 years old.

Age can also play a part. Young people tend to have greater flexibility and responsiveness to correction and change than their older counterparts. The overall health, activity level, diet and attitude each play a role. None of these factors is definitive, however.

If DCS is being addressed through the full cranial sutural procedures primarily for cosmetic purposes, and if significant health issues are not involved, the results may proceed more quickly.

Part Two

*"Your hand opens and closes, opens and closes.
If it were always a fist or always stretched open,
you would be paralyzed.
Your deepest presence is
in every small contracting and expanding,
the two as beautifully balanced and
coordinated as birds' wings."*

– Rumi

Chapter 9
Differentiating Symptoms for Diagnostic Accuracy and Healing

"You cannot judge a book by its cover."

– Cao Cao

Medical doctors are trained to diagnose their patent's disease, with great emphasis on giving the condition the proper name by way of a diagnosis. Most of the time, the official diagnosis is simply the medical term that describes the condition, and not the true cause of the ailment. If we believe the diagnosis is accurate, then applying the appropriate treatment will resolve the problem; however, the leap from diagnosis to treatment isn't always simple.

A perfect example is the ubiquitous "headache." A person suffering from headaches receives the general diagnosis of headaches or "cephalgia," which is the Latin word for head pain. The person might get more detailed about the pain experienced and receive a diagnosis of a specific type of headache, such as a cluster, migraine, tension or any of the other 150 currently recognized headache types. Just because you have a diagnosis, doesn't mean you or the doctor knows how to eliminate the cause of the pain.

According to the World Health Organization (WHO), tension-type headaches (TTH) are the most common type of headache. Their website provides a great deal of interesting headache facts including these about TTH:

- This headache is described as pressure or tightness, often like a band around the head, sometimes spreading into or from the neck.

- Its mechanism may be stress-related or associated with musculo-skeletal problems in the neck.

- TTH often begins during the teenage years, affecting three women to every two men.

- Episodic TTH, occurring on fewer than 15 days per month, is reported by more than 70 percent of some populations.

- Episodic TTH attacks usually last a few hours but can persist for several days.

- Chronic TTH, occurring on more than 15 days per month, affects one to three percent of adults.

- Chronic TTH can be unremitting and is much more disabling than episodic TTH.

A typical medical approach would be to prescribe muscle relaxants to alleviate the headache pain. But is muscle tension the real cause? As noted by WHO, the pain may be stress-related or associated with musculoskeletal problems. The key is discovering the cause of the muscle tension. To illustrate, three examples are provided below.

Patient One:

Patient One is experiencing excessive muscle tension because he has a Chiropractic Subluxation Complex called the Category II Distortion. The twist in his hips resulting from the Category II subluxation produces an uneven base for his spine to stand up straight against gravity. This hip twist causes his whole body to twist and tilt to counter the hip placement. This countering alerts the balance mechanisms of the brain. Aware of the abnormal gravitational pulls, the brain sends additional nerve signals to the muscles of the neck and shoulders to stabilize the body, causing the excess neuromuscular tension that can lead to headaches. In this case, the cause of the headaches may be the Category II subluxation complex. To correct these headaches the pelvic balance must be restored.

Patient Two:

Patient Two has also been diagnosed with tension headaches; however, she is experiencing increased muscle spasms due to worry. Her worrying creates abnormal emotional stresses and muscular tension, causing headaches. Her pain is indistinguishable from the tension headaches experienced by Patient One, even though the causes are completely different. This patient required the full Integrated Sutural Protocols to resolve her condition.

Patient Three:

Patient Three is experiencing tension headaches because of a cranial injury that caused a subluxation of her parietal bones, those generally thought of as the "top of the head." The part of the brain underneath the parietal bones governs pain and muscle function throughout the body. A cranial subluxation in the region that controls neck and shoulder muscles is creating the excess tension that is producing her headaches. To find relief, Patient Three needs her parietal bone subluxations to be corrected.

Patient Four:

Patient Four has been under tremendous stress, which has fatigued his adrenal glands. When the adrenal glands are compromised, they don't secrete enough of the proper hormones to maintain precise regulation of minerals in the body. Because of excess stress, Patient Four is suffering from an imbalance in the mineral metabolism of calcium and or magnesium. When this imbalance occurs, the result can be excess muscle tension leading to headaches. To heal and stop his headaches, Patient

Four will need to supplement the missing minerals and rehabilitate his adrenal function.

An unlimited number of possibilities can create excess muscle tension in the human body. As illustrated above, depending on the true cause of the tensions, different treatments may be required. Thus, the technical diagnosis is unlikely to lend insight into the cause or the optimal treatment for that particular individual, and a person suffering from an accurate diagnosis of a "tension-type headache" may not respond to typical treatments. An exacting intervention is required and is wholly dependent on the root cause of the headaches.

Chapter 10
Alternative Cranial Techniques

"It is a very brave choice to go against traditional medicine and embrace the alternative route."

– Suzanne Somers

The main focus of this book is on the De Jarnette Cranial Syndrome (DCS) and the full cranial sutural treatment. In the full sutural protocol, the doctor will apply a systematic intervention to address all the sutures of the cranium, treating the system as a whole for proper correction of dysfunctions.

However, many other types of cranial dysfunctions (far too many to include in this book) can occur that don't require a full sutural treatment for the patient to experience symptom relief. This chapter will provide a brief insight into these cases and the successful resolution of symptoms using alternative cranial techniques.

Case Study - Shirley

Shirley was a superb young athlete. As a teenager, she studied various forms of dance including ballet. While practicing the arabesque ballet positions, which are specific poses in ballet, she found she could perform this maneuver easily on her left leg but could not achieve the same position on her right leg.

When all orthopedic and neurological tests returned as normal, a cranial subluxation of some sort was presumed the cause. After performing a cranial examination, a temporal bone cranial subluxation was discovered. The temporal bone is on the sides of the skull behind the temples. After performing the corrective procedure to the tempo-

ral bone, her ballet positioning problem was corrected. She was able to perform a normal arabesque on her right leg immediately after treatment.

When the condition returned a few times over the course of several months, it was treated the same way. The results were identical after each treatment. Finally, the cranial subluxation stabilized, and the problem was permanently resolved. Shirley went on to study dance in college and is now a professional dancer. The problem has never resurfaced.

Bones and Brains

The brain is arranged in an organized fashion so that different areas of the brain control different functions. These areas have been thoroughly mapped and are mostly consistent from person to person. Problems with specific cranial bones can directly affect the brain area that the bone covers and protects. The temporal bone, among many other things, has an influence on coordination and proprioception.

Proprioception is the brain's ability to determine where all the body parts are at any given moment in time. Because of the temporal bone subluxation, Shirley's brain could not pinpoint the exact position of her body while standing on her right leg. The left side worked fine but the positioning messages weren't being integrated properly on both sides. The underlying neurological function normalized once the proper alignment of the cranial structures was restored giving her the ability to perform the dance maneuver.

Another dancer-patient found she could no longer execute certain moves after an automobile accident.

Case Study - Monica

Monica's car accident caused whiplash, which resolved almost completely after a series of treatments. She was free of the neck pains and spine tension she'd been experiencing. However, one mysterious problem persisted. She was unable to hold a specific ballet pose, the "Developpe a La Seconde" on one side of her body.

In this ballet pose, the dancer stands on one leg with the other foot pointing straight above her head. It looks like a standing split. On the right leg, she could execute and hold the position perfectly. She couldn't hold this pose on her left side. Each time she tried, her body would uncontrollably twist to the right.

Ballet dancers are some of the toughest athletes in the world. Countless hours of grueling training result in super-human strength, control and endurance. Monica had earned these attributes to a far greater extent than most. Still, her body would not cooperate on the left side after her car accident.

Upon further examination, Monica was suffering from a sphenobasilar subluxation. The sphenoid is a butterfly-shaped bone in the skull located behind the eyes. These important bones attach to the occipital bone, which forms the base of the skull. Improper alignment of the sphenoid bones can cause a wide variety of seemingly unrelated problems, making this type of misalignment difficult to diagnose. Like Shirley, Monica's brain was not communicating well, making the desired ballet position impossible to hold. Once the cranial subluxation was corrected and her brain was again capable of precise communication with the rest of her body, the problem immediately resolved. Twenty years hence, she has not had a recurrence.

As noted earlier in the book, the skull is composed of several bones, so the potential for misalignment of one or more of them during a person's life is great. The next three case studies involve problems caused by misalignment of the parietal bones, those that cover a large swath of the skull from the top and moving toward the back. The body's pain receptors in the brain are protected by these bones.

Case Study - Dominique

Dominique was a brilliant gymnast with world class potential. Fully aware that winning medals does not come without hard work, she put her heart and soul into everything she did. Training for that level of performance often has consequences in the form of aches, pains and injuries. Therefore, it was not surprising when Dominique came to my office with knee pain.

Usually when these young athletes have some form of injury, they know exactly when it occurred. They tend to be hyper-aware of their bodies and have developed a keen sense about their physical activities. At the same time, they are also kids who are full of energy and vitality. Sometimes injuries simply don't register until much later.

Dominique couldn't remember any injury or trauma associated with the onset of her knee pain. She just knew that it hurt with even the simplest of activities such as squatting. It didn't stop her from training, but her astute mother realized the pain was a warning from Dominique's nervous system saying that something was wrong.

Usually, a subluxation of one of the knee bones produces pain. The misalignments are adjusted back to their normal position and the problem goes away. In Dominique's case, testing the knee joints and alignments didn't uncover any abnormalities.

The next obvious step was to check her lower spine for subluxations. If a subluxation was present, it could prevent the brain's control signals from reaching the knee muscles properly. Improper communication could cause the various muscles attached to the knee to become uncoordinated, resulting in an asymmetrical motion in the knee that would hurt during activity. No subluxations were found.

This left but one place to look, her cranium. When quizzed about a possible head injury, she stated there were none that she could remember. Upon examination, a subluxation of the parietal bones was discovered. The area was tender and slightly out of place or subluxated. Interestingly, this subluxation was located exactly in the area where the brain perceives pain and controls muscle function of the knee. After correcting the cranial subluxation, Dominique could immediately perform deep knee bends without any pain.

Her injury did prove to be a bit stubborn, however. She was pain free for a week or two, but it kept returning. The same parietal bone was misaligned. After treatment, her results were identical. The pain immediately resolved. After her third visit to fix the problem, she was again asked about any head injuries.

This time she looked a bit sheepish because she remembered diving into a swimming pool and hitting the top of her head in the spot where the cranial subluxation occurred. The injury took a year to resolve. Slowly, her knee pain became less frequent and eventually completely resolved as the cranial bone was restored to and maintained its normal position.

Case Study – Peter

Peter, an intelligent, active and healthy young man in his mid-30s, suffered from musculoskeletal complaints and digestive difficulties when I first met him. He had shown great improvement with other treatments. However, he still suffered from nagging neck, shoulder, upper back and head pains, which refused to resolve.

Peter's issues had not indicated involvement of the cranium. His lack of progress on the nagging pain in his upper extremities seemed to suggest a parietal misalignment was somehow part of the remaining subluxation complex.

Upon further investigation, a significant subluxation of one of the parietal bones was found. Peter recalled a serious blow to the top of his head about 15 years earlier. It didn't affect him overtly, and he'd forgotten about it.

With nothing to lose, he agreed to a parietal bone adjustment. Correcting the misalignment was quite a challenge and took considerable time during his visit. When the treatment was over, Peter felt like a changed man. He later reported that in the days following the treatment he felt he had been relieved of a heavy burden. He felt mentally, emotionally and physically lighter. The constant companion of tension in his upper back was completely gone for a few days, and when it returned, it was not with the same intensity, nor did it last as long. While his treatment is still ongoing, there is now a reasonable expectation that his issues will be completely resolved.

Case Study – Plantar Fasciitis Experiment

To assess the success of parietal bone treatments, the outcomes of seven plantar fasciitis sufferers were documented. To participate in this unscientific study I conducted, sufferers must have tried several other solutions that had failed.

Plantar fasciitis is a condition that develops when the fascia on the bottom of the foot becomes irritated and painful. The area is inflamed and aggravated by any activity that involves the person being on their feet, making it especially difficult to resolve. Usual treatments include physical therapy, foot supports and anti-inflammatory agents. Each of the people involved in this study had unsuccessfully undergone these other therapeutic interventions. Patients ranged in age from 29 to 62 years old.

The patients varied in length of time suffering, as well as whether one or both feet were involved. Each patient received the same specific parietal bone adjustment for pain in the foot. While all seven recovered completely, one patient needed only one treatment; another required nine treatments. Overall, the average number of treatments was 3.9.

Plantar fasciitis is a difficult, frustrating, painful condition that is challenging to eliminate. This experiment suggests that cranial bone subluxation may be a cause of plantar fasciitis, and that cranial manipulation in specific areas is a viable answer for sufferers, especially when all other paths to resolution have failed.

I assisted in the treatment of these next two case studies alongside my sister Dr. Mary Unger-Boyd, who is also a Certified Craniopath.

Case Study – Meredith

Meredith was a professional softball player who had a history of head trauma. One November, during a softball game, she was hit in the back of the head with a hard-thrown softball. The impact was so great that she was knocked unconscious. When Meredith awoke, she insisted she was fine and went on to finish the game. Later that day, she was diagnosed with a severe concussion that was accompanied by painful swelling on the back of her head.

Then the problems began. She began to distance herself from people and couldn't tolerate bright lights or noise. She had periods of blurry vision and found herself struggling to put words together or follow conversations. Worst of all were the excruciating headaches that always originated from the spot where she was hit. She continued to live with these issues until another head injury pushed her to find relief.

The second injury was a softball to the face. It hit on the right side causing a hairline fracture below her eye as well as pushing in two of her teeth. As she recovered, she noticed significant sinus issues accompanied by trouble breathing. She also started having jaw pain.

Dr. Unger-Boyd performed a range of Craniopathy techniques to address the range of Meredith's problems. The frequency of her headaches decreased significantly after the first treatment. Follow-up treatments improved her vision and attention span. Meredith began to connect with life again as her symptoms — and the resulting pain — decreased.

Case Study – Brian

During a carjacking, Brian was struck forcefully in the face with the butt of the carjacker's gun. The impact fractured the maxilla, the bony structure that holds the upper teeth, on the right side of his face. Brian sought immediate medical care. The attending physician did not feel surgery was necessary to repair the damage. Instead, Brian was told the fracture would head with little structural change. It did heal but left him with some nerve damage.

A dull, throbbing ache in the affected area became Brian's constant companion. The pain began radiating into the right nasal canal and into some teeth. Each time this happened, Brian ended up in the full throes of a cluster headache.

It only took one facial adjustment by Dr. Unger-Boyd for Brian's pain to melt away. He only needed one follow-up visit to permanently resolve the pain.

In many ways, this chapter illuminates what Chiropractic Craniopaths observe daily. Everybody suffers from a head injury at some point in their lives. Yet, not every blow causes problems, and pain in the body can have many other causes. Also true is that not all pains are due to misaligned bones in the skull. However, when an unexplained pain fails to resolve or recurs, it is quite possible it's because of cranial subluxations.

Case Study – Dr. Laverne and ADD

You are probably familiar with the terms ADD and ADHD, which stand for Attention Deficit Disorder (ADD) and Attention Deficit Hyperactivity Disorder (ADHD). Current data estimate that 2-18% of our school-age children suffer from these conditions. In many of these individuals the condition follows them into later years when it is called Adult ADD.

Symptoms may include:

- *Fidgeting, squirming when seated*
- *Getting up frequently to walk or run around*
- *Running or climbing excessively when it's inappropriate (in teens and adults this may appear as restlessness)*
- *Having difficulty playing quietly or engaging in quiet leisure activities*

- *Always 'on the go'*
- *Talking excessively, frequently dominating conversations*
- *Difficulty paying attention to details and tendency to make careless mistakes in school or other activities*
- *Producing work that is often messy and careless*
- *Easily distracted by irrelevant stimuli*
- *Frequently interrupting ongoing tasks to attend to trivial distractions or events that are usually ignored by others*
- *Inability to sustain attention on tasks or activities*
- *Difficulty finishing schoolwork or paperwork or performing tasks that require concentration*
- *Frequent shifts from one uncompleted activity to another*
- *Procrastination*
- *Disorganized work habits*
- *Forgetfulness in daily activities; e.g., missing appointments, forgetting to bring lunch*
- *Failure to complete tasks such as homework or chores*
- *Frequent shifts in conversation, not listening to others, not keeping one's mind on conversations*
- *Not following details or rules of activities in social situations*

By now you are probably getting the picture. This could apply to many individuals and there are no strict diagnostic rules. Also, all the symptoms are presented in varying degrees. There also can be different manifestations depending on which experts are engaged.

Furthermore, many of these behaviors may be caused by many possible conditions, including hormonal imbalances, nutritional disturbances, learned behavior patterns and possibly cranial subluxations.

Treatments are most commonly of a pharmaceutical nature to combat the disturbing symptoms. Many other types of interventions are becoming popular. They can include diets, exercises, neurological training and a multitude of therapies that often are very useful.

An essential question still needs to be answered. What causes this disorder? Is it environmental? Is a genetic? Maybe dietary?

I and others have become convinced that there may also be a structural component, at least in some individuals, as illustrated by the experiences described below.

Dr. Laverne has lived with ADD all her life. Focusing on tasks has always been an issue. Fortunately for her she is highly intelligence and able to learn quickly, despite the constant distractions in her head. Laverne not only earned her Doctor of Chiropractic degree; she went on to earn advanced certifications in chiropractic specialties. Although ADD presented challenges in the pursuit of educational excellence, she prevailed, and her performance was exemplary. I had the pleasure to work with her for a time, and can honestly say, she is one of the best I have ever seen. And I have seen many hundreds.

Dr. Laverne is quite active. She routinely participates in extreme sports and is physically fit. Nevertheless, she experienced nagging low back pain and chronic fatigue for years, despite her excellent diet and high activity levels. She was diagnosed with the Category II subluxation complex and treated regularly. Although her low back pain was reduced after treatment, it consistently reoccurred. The non-stabilizing Category II pelvic complex, even after proper treatment procedures are performed, is one major indication of the need for the full Integrated Sutural Protocol (ISP) to address the De Jarnette Cranial Syndrome (DCS. This treatment was proposed to Dr. Laverne and

agreed. It is important to understand that, for many years, Dr. La-
verne had engaged in every conventional and nonconventional ther-
apy available to address her symptoms. Those that proved useful were
religiously continued. In other words, she was already undergoing
virtually every treatment known to be beneficial to her but still expe-
riencing significant symptoms daily.

The first application of the ISP produced amazing results. Dr. Laverne's
low back pain disappeared, seemingly magically, and remained that
way for several weeks. This was the first time in years that this com-
plaint was completely resolved. Her energy levels increased, and her
mental clarity greatly improved. She was able to focus and, seemingly
incidentally, noticed that the shape of her eyes had become even.

The shape of the orbit, the socket that the eyeball sits in, can be al-
tered with subluxations of the temporal bone. As is explained in other
chapters, the temporal bones counter-rotate in a reciprocal fashion.
One turns one way and the other turns the opposite. This is a promi-
nent feature of the DCS and is apparent in varying degrees depending
on the person. Most people do not notice this distortion, but Chiro-
practic Craniopaths and all my SOT® students frequently observe this.

Over the next several weeks, many symptoms began to slowly return.
We were able to manage the low back pain with periodic treatment of
the Category II subluxation complex, but the pain would recur. Diffi-
culty with focus and the other adult ADD symptoms crept back into
the picture. A second ICS was performed. The following describes the
results of this treatment in the doctor's own words.

>   *"Dr. Joe-*
>   *Here are the things I noticed within the first 12 -24 hours*
>   *after the sutural procedure....*

I got sleepy (lots of yawning) immediately after, but my mind felt alert. The tired feeling lasted about two hours. I also felt like I had a balloon head. Literally it felt like my brain had more room to float around.

My plan was to go home and take a nap, but I started to feel like I wanted to be productive. I ended up running errands, doing laundry, cleaning, etc. I was on the go till about 9pm. Lately I have been lethargic and must give myself a pep talk to get anything done, so this was a nice change.

I slept really well and deeply. When I got up it was easier than the last few weeks. My mood felt elevated and I wasn't so sluggish. When I was putting my makeup on, I noticed my left eye was more symmetrical to my right. This is similar to what happened after my first sutural procedure.

I haven't done anything to test my brain focus yet, but I have lots of studying to do today. I will keep you updated.

Thanks again for the killer sutural procedure...it is much appreciated!"

The effects of this treatment continued like the previous ones. Dr. Laverne was studying for one of her advanced certifications and found her brain focused and clear once again. If only these treatments were available to her 20 years earlier, it would have saved countless hours of needless hard work and frustration. Still, she learned empathy for others with this condition, an experience that is priceless for a physician: to truly understand what the patient is going through.

Once again, her symptoms improved quite dramatically, and this time, they were maintained for a longer period. As expected, she was not perfectly cured yet. The next application of the ICS proved to be *invaluable to all involved. This time there was another doctor present, and I was partially explaining the procedure during its application. In other chapters you will learn of the importance of focus and intent, not only by the patient or anyone intent upon achieving desired goals in life, but also for the doctor in the proper application of the ICS. During the treatment I neglected this one essential aspect of the procedure. My focus was divided.*

Without proper focus and intent, the treatment was more mechanical in nature. It lacked the depth and finesse that total focus and intent bring to this procedure. If we think about it, this is no different than any other intricate activity in life. A sporting competition, a concert violinist, a racecar driver and so on. Optimal success at any precision activity requires total concentration and focus.

Interestingly, Dr. Laverne reported that her low back pain improved significantly. However, the mental components of her condition were largely unchanged following the treatment. She experienced no improvement in mental clarity or ability to concentrate and study. The orbit size remained uneven when she applied makeup. This proved to be an invaluable lesson to all of us. This treatment resulted in the physical changes but failed to produce the deeper ones.

Dr. Laverne experienced the treatment as being identical to the previous applications. She had no prior conceptions suggesting that my treatment would have different effects than previous ones. Because she is a very accurate and reliable reporter of the how her brain functions, I find her reporting of this experience invaluable.

I judged this intervention to be a partial failure, and the ISP was again applied. This time the results were much like the previous ones. Orbit size changed immediately, as did focus, clarity and head pres-

sures. All the symptoms remained improved for even a longer period of time than the previous treatments.

Dr. Laverne subsequently moved out of the area and is in practice in a different part of the country. She receives glowing reports from her patients and continues exemplary work. It has been over a year at this writing, and she reports significant improvement in her overall condition compared to previous decades.

This case illustrates the experiences of many patients and practitioners. Proper diagnosis of the De Jarnette Cranial Syndrome (DCS) and thorough treatment by the Integrated Sutural Protocol (ISP) can prove to be an invaluable component in the treatment of ADD and ADHD.

Chapter 11
Occipital Fibers and Temporomandibular Dysfunction (TMD)

All things are bound together. All things connect.
— Chief Seattle

Earlier in Chapter 3 occipital fibers were mentioned. These tiny fibers are located on the back of the head and were originally discovered by Dr. M.B. De Jarnette. He found that these fibers have the reflexes related to vertebrae in the spine and eventually to the function of the organ associated with that specific vertebra.

We have seen how the brain and the human cranium affects the entire rest of the body. I would be remiss to not include some discussion as to how the rest of the body reflexively affects the cranium. The cranium is thoroughly interconnected with every aspect of human function.

In the 1930s, Dr. M.B. De Jarnette began reporting his research concerning what he then termed the suboccipital fibers. His research went on to include the occipital fibers. Integrating his research with other pioneers in anatomy and neurology, he developed an understanding of how these tiny fibers and muscles affect human physiology. Part of his research was conducted by Arthur C. Guyton MD, the author of *Guyton's Physiology*.

While this account is not reported in the mainstream medical history books, it was confirmed by my students several years ago at Logan University. They tracked down Dr. Guyton, then retired, and personally spoke to him about his research concerning the occipital fibers. His anatomical and neurological findings contributed to the scientific basis of De Jarnette's findings.

De Jarnette concluded that these fibers react to a multitude of neurological influences throughout the body, including the organ systems. He found them to have reflexes related to specific vertebrae in the spine and eventually to the function of the organ associated with that specific vertebra.

Currently new research has rediscovered and renamed these fibers as the *myodural bridge* and the *rectus capitus posterior minor muscles*. Some of this groundbreaking research is being performed by Dr. Dennis Ennis, of Logan University in St. Louis, and others. The mainstream approach to therapy is focused on treating the muscles of the back of the neck; however, this approach does not fully appreciate the interconnectedness of these tiny fibers with other parts of the body and the relationships to functional neurology.

The research is becoming more popularized, and more mainstream therapists are now treating these muscles with massage techniques. Sadly, they only address the muscle tension which is the end product of a much different problem.

These little fibers react to nerve impulses that can be generated by a stressed organ in the body. The organ can be stressed by nerve blockage from the spine, mental or emotional stress, nutritional deficiencies and imbalances and/or diseases and medical conditions.

When an organ is overstressed, whether or not we feel any symptoms, the body reacts by sending signals to the brain. Under the proper circumstances, these signals will trigger a reaction into the occipital fiber. This fiber can swell and produce a constant pull or tug upon the base of the skull called the occipital bone.

This fiber may become swollen or tender, or it can also go undetected for years or decades. It can, however, be the cause of headaches or other alterations in cranial function. It can impede normal cranial bone motion, which is essential for proper brain and nervous system function.

It may also produce cranial distortions that can produce cranial nerve dysfunction.

Occipital Fibers and Temporomandibular Dysfunction (TMD): A Case Study

One such demonstration of this theory presented itself at a seminar I taught some years ago. It illustrates the relationship between organ function and the cranium, as well as the complexity of temporomandibular joint dysfunction (TMD). The seminar was a training program in Chiropractic Manipulative Reflex Technique (CMRT). These are the specific SOT® procedures that address the organ relationships to the spine and to the cranium.

With absolutely no idea what to expect, a doctor was chosen from the audience who experienced TMJ pains for several years. The doctor was analyzed by a diagnostic measure called a Neurometer CPT. This measures nerve function and produces similar results to a nerve conduction test. The trigeminal nerve was evaluated and found to have deficiencies on the side of his TMJ complaints.

The trigeminal nerve comes out of a little hole in the cranium from the brain and is joined by additional nerves from the upper neck. Together they produce the nerve that controls jaw muscle function and sensation.

The doctor/patient was then analyzed for occipital fiber dysfunctions as per standard SOT® procedures. He indeed had an active fiber that was connected to the function of the large intestines. The treatment protocol was applied and included CMRT reflexes for the large intestines. No other treatments were applied for this experimental intervention.

The test for trigeminal nerve function was immediately applied again with the patient still lying on the table. Performing the colon (large intestine) reflexes alone alleviated tension into the occipital fiber system at the base of the skull. This allowed the cranial structures to destress enough to take pressure off the cranial nerve and the upper cervical spine. The deficient trigeminal nerve dysfunction was found immediately improved with this examination.

Please refer to **Appendix F** for the actual, official report describing the before-and-after response to the organ reflexes treatment.

Chapter 12
Fibromyalgia

"The greatest evil is physical pain."

~ Saint Augustine

Fibromyalgia (FM) is one of the most difficult illnesses to understand and diagnose afflicting humans today. According to the National Fibromyalgia Association, 10 million people in the U.S. are afflicted with this chronic pain condition. Fibromyalgia disproportionately targets women, anywhere from 75-90 percent, although men and children can be affected, too.

Fibromyalgia sufferers typically experience widespread pain throughout their bodies. Often the pain is described as throbbing, shooting, deep and stabbing. Many sufferers also have trouble sleeping, resulting in extreme fatigue, sensitivity to touch, sound and/or light, and memory or cognitive difficulties. Other conditions can manifest, including irritable bowel syndrome, arthritis and lupus.

BioEnergy Patches are a safe, energetically based, nontoxic intervention that has proven to be exceptionally effective for many stubborn conditions, including fibromyalgia. Healing vibrations are embedded into skin patches to facilitate the body's natural healing process and they don't interfere with other medications or therapies. Of the 60+ patches currently available, those most commonly effective for the treatment of fibromyalgia are:

- Fibromyalgia – General therapy patch for fibromyalgia.
- Stress/Anxiety – Helps in coping with anxiety, stress and depression; promotes a calming effect.

- Healing XL – Enhances and accelerates the healing effects of all energy patches.
- Biofilms – Dissolves biofilms (sticky bacteria), which may reduce inflammation and edema.
- Cleanse – Promotes general cleansing.
- D-Tox – Assists with detoxification of environmental toxins.
- Heavy Metal Plus (HM) – Detoxifies with extra emphasis on heavy metals.
- Ultra Joint Plus – Promotes relief of joint symptoms; pain and inflammation; relieves headaches, trauma, acute injury, migraines and provides general pain relief.
- Energy Balance – Increases energy and boosts general healing.
- Gravity Balance – Aids and restores the body's healing function.
- Sleep – Helps to restore the normal sleep cycle.

It is recommended that a maximum of three or four therapy patches be worn at any given time. It's felt that the physical healing that must take place limits the number of patches that can be worn at any time. However, energy therapy patches have been researched and used extensively in parts of Europe. Some clinics there have noted impressive therapeutic outcomes using many more patches at the same time than recommended above. Therefore, recommendations may be influenced by your individual response and the experience of practitioners.

Fibromyalgia Symposium

In 2005, an innovative symposium focusing on fibromyalgia was held in Kansas City, Missouri, sponsored by the Sacro Occipital Research Society International, Inc. (SORSI). The goal of the conference was to gain insight into the causes of fibromyalgia and identify the most promising treatment options. Leading authorities in fibromyalgia from around the country presented their research and professional experiences at this three-day event.

All participants could attend every session and thereby learn from the totality of accumulated wisdom and information from all presenters. The group at large undertook the task of critically evaluating the knowledge presented, analyzing it for consistent themes and incongruent information. The final session of the symposium provided a forum for all the participants to contribute their knowledge, research and professional experiences to the accumulated body of information presented, thus allowing everyone to contribute to the conclusions and benefit from the experiences of each attendee and presenter.

Symposium Conclusions

Two key conclusions were reached in the symposium.

1. From a structural/neurological perspective, fibromyalgia is likely associated with a Category II or a Category III subluxation complex, or a combination of these two dysfunctions. Both involve serious structural alignment issues and neurological consequences.

2. An underlying systemic hypersensitivity exists in fibromyalgia that must be addressed. For maximum response to treatment, both the identified subluxation complex plus the hypersensitivity issues must be treated concurrently, since each aggravates the other.

These conclusions were based on many factors; however, the following illustrates some of the reasoning involved.

Fibromyalgia and Category II

The Category II subluxation complex as described earlier in this book involves sacroiliac instability, as well as proprioceptive dysfunction of the nervous system. The proprioceptive system is responsible for monitoring precise information about the position of all the body parts. When disturbed by the Category II subluxation, the body cannot tell exactly where all the parts are located. To compensate for this imbalance, the brain tells all the muscles to tighten, producing undue tension and pain, resulting in a degradation of the overall vitality of the healing systems, due to the disturbances created in the CSRM.

Dysfunction of the Category II mechanism also results in specific mechanical stresses upon the human structural system. In other words, specific areas of muscle and ligament connections tend to work harder, and therefore become inflamed and more tender to the touch. It turns out that tender points used to diagnose fibromyalgia are similar and in relative proximity to the exact stress patterns produced by the Category II subluxation complex. Because so many of these stress points coincide so closely, it is theorized that an intimate relationship exists between the Category II distortion and fibromyalgia.

Many individuals suffer from the Category II subluxation complex, and its manifestations are unique and varied. As stated previously, not everyone with the Category II problem experiences the same symptoms; therefore, the subluxation complex does not alone account for fibromyalgia. There is another necessary component, specifically some form of systemic hypersensitivity or hyperinflammatory dysfunction or additional Category III complications.

Fibromyalgia and Category III

The Category III subluxation complex includes structural distortions that compromise the function of the human cranium, stressing the parietal bones. The parietal bones cover the parietal lobes, which is the area of the brain that is responsible for all sensation in the body. Therefore, if the Category III subluxation complex is involved, it produces hypersensitivity of sensation throughout the entire body, resulting from increased pressure on the related areas of the brain.

If the fibromyalgia patient is suffering from a Category III distortion with significant parietal bone compression that produces neurological effects on the sensory and motor homunculus of the brain, proper cranial treatment is essential. Without the proper intervention, complete resolution of this condition may not be possible.

Fibromyalgia and Systemic Hypersensitivity

Another component of fibromyalgia is a systemic hypersensitivity and/or hyperinflammatory state. This aspect of the disease may require dietary, nutritional and other healing treatments such as detoxification. While many of these interventions can be done at home, to optimize healing potential, FM sufferers should also include Category II and/or Category III treatments.

Fibromyalgia Clinical Trials

With the support of SORSI and the SORSI research associates, my team and I have conducted FM treatment clinical trials. To date, the research studies have been limited to SOT treatment procedures for Category II and III, with related SOT Chiropractic Craniopathic treatments only. No additional supplementation or alternative treatments were given during the study periods, apart from the use of a sacroiliac belt, which has been found to be essential in the effective treatment of the Category II problem. The results, thus far, have been most promising and, in some cases, remarkable.

Once the studies ended, all fibromyalgia patients were introduced to nutritional support, proper supplementation, etc. Patients experienced even greater improvement with these added measures.

Fibromyalgia can be a complicated and often devastating condition; however, it is highly treatable with the proper interventions. The results from our clinical studies underscore the need for chiropractic intervention in the effective treatment of fibromyalgia.

Basic Self-Help for Fibromyalgia

Experience and research have identified many interventions that are consistently beneficial for FM sufferers, many of which can be done at home safely and effectively. The most consistently useful home therapies are described below:

1. Eliminate all refined sugars, carbohydrates, and all types of processed and canned foods. Avoid artificial colors and flavors.
2. Increase dietary intake of raw fruits, vegetables and whole grains.
3. Implement a tolerable form of daily exercise. The most valuable activities include stretching and aerobic activity. A minimum of three sessions per week is recommended; however, daily is better.
4. Include massage, yoga, Pilates or some other structurally based activity, if tolerable.
5. Consider wearing a sacroiliac belt to help stabilize the sacrum.
6. Include a daily antioxidant nutritional supplement.
7. Include an Omega-3 oil supplement. Research supports including Omega-3s for hyperinflammatory conditions. The current recommendation is 3000-4000 mg per day from a high quality, wild caught, mercury-free source (typically not the kind available at your local big box or discount store). Many individuals, for whom supplementation is needed, experience significant improvements within about a month. To determine the full effect, a trial of at least three months must be completed for accurate determination of improvement.

Below are additional considerations and suggestions to address issues often experienced by FM sufferers.

Addressing Suboptimal Organ Function

Some individuals will experience suboptimal functioning of one or more organ systems. To identify the most effective interventions for this situation, one should consult a SORSI-certified SOT specialist who is skilled in occipital fiber analysis and diagnosis. Such physicians are trained to identify these types of dysfunctions in the body and can design an effective treatment program.

Autoimmune Dysfunction

FM sufferers may also have some degree of autoimmune dysfunction. This type of disease process can often be effectively treated by using the protocol that was outlined by Dr. Royal Lee. Utilizing specially designed protomorphogens (PMGs), these conditions can often respond quite favorably. One must consult a physician experienced in protomorphology and autoimmune dysfunction to accurately evaluate and treat these situations.

Functional Blood Analysis

Standard screening blood tests can uncover hidden organ dysfunctions. However, it is imperative that the laboratory values revealed are matched to physiological optimal ranges, rather than the statistical averages used by most physicians. Statistical averages frequently mask real, solvable problems, while subclinical or hidden dysfunctions affecting a person's FM condition are often discovered using a wider blood values range. Such specialized analysis is warranted in complicated or unresponsive conditions.

Food Allergies

FM can be exacerbated by hidden food allergies or dietary sensitivities. A full panel of possible triggers can be conducted, but an easier approach is a simple saliva test that gives insight into sensitivities to four major food groups: milk protein (casein), soy, grains and eggs.

Detoxification

Detoxification can be an effective added treatment for fibromyalgia patients, if it is undertaken in a slow, measured and gentle fashion. The following are recommended detoxification methods.

- An electronic ionic foot bath effectively extracts many toxic materials from the bloodstream. Numerous patients have experienced impressive results with this procedure.

- Nutritionally supported detoxification will reduce unpleasant side effects and allow the body to rid itself of unwanted toxins in a gentle manner.

- Chelation therapy is necessary in stubborn situations and with patients who have extreme circulatory difficulties. Chelation involves the insertion of a solution into the bloodstream to attract, attach to and systematically remove heavy metals and excess minerals.

The ABC's of Energy Therapy

Many patients experience positive outcomes utilizing energy therapy to supplement the other structural, nutritional and adjunctive therapies to treat their fibromyalgia. As its name suggests, energy therapy taps into the energetic vibrational system used by the body to coordinate healing functions. Investigators in this field have determined methods of identifying some of the precise vibrational frequencies used by the body to maintain functions and stimulate healing.

AlphaBio Centrix (ABC) Energy Patches are one form of energy healing that has shown positive effects for those who are suffering from Category II and Category III subluxations. However, there are many uses for energy patches beyond these two conditions. It is worth providing a brief introduction into the structure, function and protocol of this healing modality.

I have been fascinated by the concept of energy medicine for most of my life. While I was an undergraduate premedical student, the official course of study was zoology with a minor in chemistry; however, I loved physiology and medicine so much, that after a full work week during summer breaks, I volunteered nights and weekends at the local hospital emergency room to gain experience.

The interns and doctors I met there invited me to observe surgeries, which piqued my interest in becoming a surgeon. They also proved zealous in their belief that the best doctors were those who understood physiology and chemistry, inside and out. I took their advice to heart and studied these subjects diligently.

A series of serendipitous events redirected my life down an entirely different path, simultaneously leaving me with a complete loss of faith in my chosen career: the study of Western medicine. Lost, disenchanted and directionless, I had no idea what I was going to do with the rest of my life. I knew I wanted to help people and wanted to be a physician, but traditional medicine was no longer my pre-ordained path. I had developed a philosophical crisis. Fortunately for me, I discovered the world of alternative healing systems.

Until that moment in time, I was of the belief that the allopathic medical system was the only method of healing. I was astonished to find that there were countless approaches developed throughout millennia that proposed systems of analysis and intervention for most conditions and disease processes. Furthermore, I experienced a multitude of serendipitous meetings with people reporting recoveries from many illnesses, often life-threatening, by alternative means after the traditional medical interventions failed.

It was an entirely new idea that there were mechanisms in the body that keep us healthy, and that these mechanisms are ultimately responsible for healing. If one had a method of analyzing defects in the healing mechanism, one could also devise treatments to restore the natural healing ability of the organism. I embarked upon an extensive self-study program covering a wide range of healing systems, including homeopathy, herbology, naturopathy, acupuncture, psychotherapy, hypnosis and other modes of therapy.

I was utterly amazed and intrigued by the depth and breadth of the constructs of health and healing, as found in many age-old systems, such as chiropractic, acupuncture, homeopathy and others. Eventually I came to understand that all major systems throughout history have postulated that the ultimate healing power in a living organism is energetic in nature. Each healing discipline has its own set of methods of analyzing for imbalances and dysfunctions, as well as their own unique techniques for restoring energy flow and balance, thus promoting healing. Acupuncture was unique in its constructs that describe the interplay among all the factors that can affect human health. These include mental, emotional, physical and spiritual. They include the environment, family life, relationships, diet, etc.

I was mesmerized by everything about acupuncture; however, not knowing the Chinese language, I could not imagine becoming an acupuncturist. It just so happens that the healing constructs of energy flow, blockage and balance are extremely similar in chiropractic philosophy.

As luck would have it, there was a chiropractic college in town, and I enrolled immediately.

Throughout Chiropractic College, and over four decades of clinical practice, I was consistently intrigued and often surprised by the effects of various energetic healing treatments. I, along with some of my colleagues, often built, tested and personally used a variety of energetic healing devices. I would try virtually anything to see how it worked, but after many years, found myself consistently disappointed. Because the healing energy is difficult, if not impossible to measure reliably, it is nearly impossible to determine what is wrong with a person energetically and what to do about it. All the various energetic healing devices would produce occasional effects that were seemingly miraculous, but none produced consistent results.

Because of my unflagging interest, I found myself the target of countless solicitations by companies, individuals and patients who either experienced a positive effect or wanted me to buy or sell their products. Because the success rates, in my limited experience, did not rise to my expectations, I came to ignore the great majority of all these energy-based treatments.

Then Larry became a patient. He originally presented with a serious degenerative eye condition, called uveitis, that results in blindness if untreated. He had been on oral cortisone for a decade to contain this disease. Once we determined that the cause of the problem was a subluxation of his cranial bones, following treatment, he was able to stop the medication. The symptoms of this degenerative eye disease disappeared. It has remained resolved for well over a decade at this writing.

However, because of the long-term steroid use, his immune system was severely compromised. He suffered a serious case of systemic Candida albicans, often referred to as simply "Candida." This is a fungal infection that is normal in the intestinal tract, but when it gets into the other tissues of the body it can be devastating. Larry's case was so severe that the fungus saturated his entire body and was coming out of the beds of his fingernails. It looked like spider webs where cuticles should be and was so painful that he could not touch anything with his fingers.

Larry was extremely diligent about everything concerning his health. Candida can become a serious problem, and he had exhausted all imaginable measures and interventions that he could find. He was impeccable with his diet, and had applied homeopathic, nutritional, herbal, and medical treatments for this condition. He had done the pharmaceutical interventions, and none of these treatments resolved the Candida infestation.

His wife was his health treatment scout. She suggested different things to try and insisted that he kept the faith and search for solutions. She was the one who first discovered the Energy Patches. She designed a treatment program for Larry, and within just a couple of weeks, the pain had subsided enough for him to perform all normal activities with his hands. Over the next couple of months his Candida infestation totally resolved where all other treatments had failed.

Seeing this amazing transformation of healing firsthand, I had to investigate and understand this phenomenon, especially if I were to consider providing these products to my patients. Over the next several months I recommended hundreds of these "patches" to scores of patients to determine their effectiveness. To my delight and surprise, most people enjoyed a surprisingly high success rate of resolution of symptoms and conditions, where many treatments, oftentimes over several years, had failed. Using them myself, I even began to feel relief from certain issues that I struggled with for most of my life.

Due to the high degree of success I witnessed for myself and my patients, as well as reports from many practitioners around the world, I continued to delve into the philosophy and theories concerning these products. I needed to understand how they worked or at least have a plausible working model for the effects that we were witnessing.

To this end, I synthesized information from a variety of sources. This research has been done at various places by various individuals around the world over nearly 100 years now; none of this information is available in any single location. My intent was to arrive at an integrated theory as to how and why the AlphaBio Centrix Energy Patches work.

I'll begin with some of the studies by Dr. Royal Rife, a microbiologist in the early 1900's. He developed the world's most powerful light microscope in the 1930's. No one has been able to improve upon that design yet. In many ways, he was a Renaissance man, a genius and well ahead of his time.

Dr. Rife became fascinated with the concept of destroying bacteria and viruses using vibratory frequencies. He asked someone to build a cathode ray tube for him, which is essentially like a TV set that emits a beam of electromagnetic radiation. It was designed such that he could tune in the specific vibration of electromagnetic frequencies to be emitted.

Unlike the television, which had not yet been invented, it emitted a single particle beam. The old traditional tube television is designed to scan lines across the surface, producing little light flashes on the screen at the rate of thousands of times a second. The intent of Rife's cathode ray machine was to project specific vibratory frequencies at bacteria and viruses using a single beam.

He discovered that when he identified the precise frequency of vibrations that resonated with a specific bacteria or virus, it would kill that bacteria or virus. Through access to YouTube, it is possible to view some of the original footage of Dr. Rife's projects. One of his important research projects was with tuberculosis, a scourge of his day. You can watch the tuberculosis bacteria under the microscope and, after 10 to 15 seconds of exposure to the cathode ray tube emissions, the organism splits open and dies. In the videos available, Dr. Rife was projecting the cathode ray beam through 15 feet of cement from the basement of his laboratory to get to the microscope.

While Dr. Rife's studies using the cathode ray tube for this purpose were limited, he did produce the Rife machine to treat various conditions. Dr. Rife proposed that if one could obtain the exact frequencies needed by the body, it could then assist in the healing those conditions.

I know several people who own these machines, and I have had several patients experience good results with a variety of ailments utilizing the Rife machine. Sometimes seemingly miraculous results occur. This technology has merit but does not produce consistently positive results. I think there are several reasons for this. Dr. Rife's machine produces three vibratory frequencies at a time. But people and their conditions are far too complicated and complex to respond to three simple vibrational frequencies. Still, the fact that the machine works to the extent that it does, illustrates a revolutionary concept in healing and still astounds me. The videos of some of his experiments are truly compelling.

Another researcher in the early days of exploration in energetic healing was a Russian doctor named Georges Lakhovsky. He initially observed how homing pigeons became disoriented around radio towers. This observation, along with other research, led him to deduce that there was some internal homing mechanism that was being interfered with by the radio waves, and that these homing mechanisms in the brain could be affected by vibratory frequencies of a certain range. Eventually his research, and that of several others, discovered that the band of electromagnetic healing frequencies is in the gigahertz range. This coincides perfectly with those used in the ABC energy patches.

Interestingly, Dr. Lakhovsky reported this approximately 100 years ago, and went on to conduct a series of fascinating experiments. Lakhovsky eventually postulated that every cell, every part of every cell, each system, organ and even every organelle within cells, formed oscillatory vibratory circuits. In other words, they were like tiny musical instruments. They emitted an array of vibrations unique unto each structure.

This symphony of vibratory emissions from all the body parts formed resonant patterns that ultimately had an essential role in the function of physiology, biochemistry and the healing process. These are very real and discrete vibratory patterns. They are measurable, actual electromagnetic energy patterns in the physical world. They are very tiny and difficult to measure, but they do exist.

This is further evidenced by the following excerpt available through www.mercola.com. The research team led by Dr. Henrik Mouritsen of the University of Oldenburg in Germany published their study in the May 2014 issue of the journal *Nature*.

> For the first time, scientists have revealed that average levels of electromagnetic noise, or "electro smog," completely disrupt the magnetic compass of migratory robins. This is true even when the electromagnetic signal levels are just 1/1000th of the limit which the World Health Organization (WHO) defines as harmless.
>
> Electro smog is the unseen electromagnetic radiation that is generated from the use of both wireless technology and household electricity. Common sources of electro smog include utility smart meters, cell towers and antennae, cell phones, cordless phones, wireless Internet routers, microwaves, high voltage transmission lines, baby monitors and other wireless devices including WIFI, computers, monitors, laptops, tablets, reading devices, computer monitors, wired and wireless cell phone headsets, and educational interactive whiteboards. (Nature, May 15, 2014, Issue 509, pp 353-356)

The AlphaBio Centrix Energy Therapy Patches (ABC) deliver essential vibratory frequencies and patterns that are missing or deficient in sick or ailing organisms. It is theorized that when an organ, structure or system becomes sick, it may lose the ability to produce the full array of essential vibratory energies; therefore, it also loses its ability to reintegrate with the rest of the body, and healing is sacrificed.

The pioneer and researcher, Richard Eaton and his co-developer, the late Dr. Ricky Hunt, developed methods to analyze sick individuals for missing or deficient energetic frequencies within the specific range of the healing spectrum. By evaluating numerous individuals with similar conditions, he could identify consistent energetic signatures associated with that disease process.

Next, they engineered a method for embedding these specific discrete frequencies into patches that can be worn on the skin. Not unlike the Rife machine in this aspect, they are different in that up to 33 discrete vibrational patterns can be embedded into an ABC Energy Patch. Furthermore, it is found that up to three different patches can be used at any given time and will often synergize with each other, enhancing effectiveness. Instead of 1 to 3 frequencies as projected by the Rife machine, the patches will deliver approximately 100 or more separate and discrete frequencies and can be worn 24 hours a day for seven days a week. This is accomplished by using up to 3-4 different AlphaBio Centrix (ABC) Energy Therapy Patches at a time.

The ABC therapies deliver an array of precise vibrational frequencies that are designed to help supply energetic deficiencies in an ailing system. I have witnessed amazing results in many conditions by hundreds of individuals. Of course, nothing works on everyone, but the ABC therapies have the extremely convincing benefits from my experience.

This is a very brief overview of a very complicated subject. A one-hour video lecture available on YouTube entitled "The Scientific Basis of

Energetic Healing" gives a bit more detailed information concerning this subject which, in my opinion, truly deserves greater investigation. This video is presented in four segments and includes a recording of my presentation at the 7th International Medical Conference of Bio-Cybernetic and Energy Medicine held in St Louis, Mo. in 2011. The full four-hour version was presented at a SORSI (Sacro Occipital Research Society International, Inc.) conference and is available through www.SORSI.com

Chapter 13
Detoxification

"Cleansing is like my meditation. It makes me stop,
focus and think about what I'm putting into my body.
I'm making a commitment to my health
and hitting the reset button."
– Salma Hayek

The road to optimal health, while highly individualized, is built upon the bedrock of core principles common to all humankind. Paramount among these principles is the concept of detoxification. As global warming illustrates, we live in an increasingly toxic world. The accumulation of these poisons undoubtedly has serious effects on human health, as well as all organisms on the planet.

During my undergraduate studies in pre-medical school in the early 1970s, I discovered a report by the American Cancer Association which concluded that at least 90 percent of cancers were due to environmental toxins. The report's recommendation was to develop a vaccine to prevent people from getting cancer when exposed to these various toxins. While some skeptics would argue that scientific literature is inconclusive with respect to human toxicity and its relationship to disease, this conclusion has serious flaws. One of the most important embraces the concept of synergy.

Synergistic Effects

The definition of synergy is two or more agents that together have a greater impact than each does separately. For example, most people can drink a couple of beers without any negative repercussions. They can likewise take a prescription-sized dose of barbiturates for some ailment without serious consequence. However, if the two are combined, the mixture can prove deadly because the synergistic effect of these two substances together is much greater than a simple summation of the two effects.

The FDA currently allows untold thousands of manmade, toxic substances into the air we breathe, the food we eat and the water we drink. Not only is it impossible to predict the effects of the combination of all these different ingredients; it is even more difficult to predict their effects upon a given individual.

Components of Detoxification

Most cleansing procedures target specific components of detoxification. In her groundbreaking book, *Clinical Purification*, Gina L. Nick, Ph.D., N.D. illustrates that detoxification is a complex, multi-step venture requiring intervention at various levels. In order to cleanse the system fully, it must begin at the intracellular level. If a toxic substance is trapped within cells and structures, such as the nervous system, bone, liver, etc., attempts to rid the body of toxins will be compromised until the toxic substances are extracted from those structures. The essential avenues of exit include the skin, lungs, colon, liver and kidneys.

To function optimally, these various structures require the appropriate nutrition, nerve supply and vital energy. When one or more of these requirements is missing or compromised, the ability to detoxify is diminished. For example, a spinal misalignment can result in decreased nerve energy to the kidneys, which inhibits how they function and detoxify. If a cranial distortion affects the pituitary gland, the individual may not sweat normally causing inefficiency in skin detoxification. Another individual may be deficient in a micronutrient or trace mineral. The deficiency inhibits liver or colon function, resulting in improper detoxification.

Detoxification — or elimination — is one of five essential steps in the nutritional process. These steps are:

1. Ingestion
2. Digestion
3. Absorption
4. Assimilation
5. Elimination

Improper function of any of the first four will result in compromised detoxification.

Finally, the overall vitality of the person is an important component in the detoxification process. If a person has low vitality, his body is going to be less likely to have the appropriate energetic resources to detoxify optimally. Before detoxification can occur, an improvement in the overall vitality must occur or the detoxification process will be suboptimal.

Determining Toxicity Levels

Certain diagnostic methods, such as hair or saliva analysis, can sometimes give insights into the levels of certain specific toxic compounds in the body. An accurate assessment of the degree of overall toxicity a person may be experiencing is difficult at best. Be aware that any technology proposing to evaluate a level of toxicity for the human body does not necessarily predict the impact of that toxicity on any given individual. Some people are highly sensitive to even the smallest amounts of certain toxins. Therefore, some migraines can be triggered by simply smelling gasoline while filling the gas tank. Conversely, in rare instances, very toxic levels may not seem to affect the health of certain individuals much at all. This phenomenon explains how a heavy smoker can live to be well into her nineties.

A simple, yet effective means of judging how well a detoxification program is working is how you feel after it's over. A simple assessment can be done before and after to gauge the success of the detox. This method is subjective, but how you feel is subjective, too. If you feel better after the initial detoxification program, then toxicity levels may be affecting your well-being. This would indicate that an ongoing detoxification program is warranted.

If, on the other hand, you experience no positive effect from the program, then you may need to look further to boost your level of health or address specific symptoms or conditions. Even so, engaging in some form of routine detoxification is an essential aspect of a good prevention program to enhance optimal health.

General Detoxification

Many programs have a one-size-fits-all approach to detoxification. This approach can fail because every person is unique and will respond to detoxification differently. A variety of approaches may be necessary for each person to detoxify completely. There are several general detoxification approaches; a few are listed here:

Fasting

Fasting is a time-honored approach to detoxification, and many people have reported extraordinary results from an extended fast. At one time, fasting clinics existed throughout Europe. The relief many reported after fasting from often debilitating conditions was amazing.

A true fast is a mental, emotional, physical and even spiritual experience. Ideally, fasting is best done during low-stress periods. Given the busyness of the modern life, fasting tends to be impractical. If undertaken, it is best to work with a qualified professional to monitor progress, especially if you are new to the process.

There are many ways to conduct a fast. Here are some of the most common.

Dry fasting is an extreme type of fast, which has the practitioner foregoing food and water for short periods. Dry fasting is rooted in spirituality and is not something to consider without the counsel of a physician. Experts are often reluctant to suggest a dry fast because it can release too many toxins into the bloodstream too quickly leaving the body unable to discharge them easily. As a result, the individual may experience undue discomfort, if not damage, from the inability to excrete all the toxins being released.

Liquid fasting allows only for liquids. Below are the most common liquid fasts.

- Water fasting is the simplest form of liquid fasting. It is considered a true therapeutic fast as detoxification happens rapidly. However, it can be difficult to adhere to the "water only" rule as detox symptoms manifest. It is not suggested as the first option for someone new to fasting.

- Juice fasting offers some nutritional support delivered from juiced fruits and/or vegetables.

- The Master Cleanse or Lemonade Diet became popular in the 1970s. Pure maple syrup provides calories during the fast. The goal of this fast is intestinal cleansing.

- Partial fasting, also known as selective fasting, includes some solid food. The amount of food varies, as the goal is to exclude or limit certain foods rather than refraining from all foods. An example of a partial fast is a cleansing diet.

Just as there are many types of fasts, the time spent fasting also varies. Key considerations on fast length include experience with fasting, goals for fasting and the nutritional reserves already in place.

- A 24-hour fast is recommended for beginners as it's enough time to make a difference, but not so much time that unpleasant detox symptoms start. A 24-hour fast may stave off sickness if done as soon as symptoms begin, as it encourages the body's resources to focus on fighting off the illness.

- A three-day fast is a good monthly maintenance routine that will keep toxins cleansed on a regular basis.

- A one-week fast can be used as a quarterly or seasonal detox.

- A 10-day fast is the recommended length for a Master Cleanse fast. This timeframe is also suitable as a yearly maintenance detox.

- A multi-week fast is only for seasoned fasters or those under professional supervision because you must know your body and its reactions to the fasting process.

Fasting can provide cleansing benefits and allow for greater understanding of the body and its reactions to detoxification. As noted above, it's best to attempt fasts during low-stress periods and with the supervision of physician or other experienced personnel.

Sauna/Infrared Sauna

Traditional steam saunas and the newer, steam free infrared saunas do the same thing. They increase body heat, which is known to have certain therapeutic effects. Detoxification also occurs through the enhanced sweating done in a sauna. Some individuals experience significant-to-profound improvements by utilizing routine saunas.

Massage/Lymphatic Drainage

The lymphatic system is somewhat analogous to the sidewalks and back alleyways of city housing. All the trash and garbage exit down these pathways. Since the lymph system is also intimately involved with immunity, such procedures can certainly facilitate generalized detoxification. Again, the effectiveness can best be determined by engaging in a series of treatments to evaluate any changes you may experience.

Specific Detoxification

Liver/Gall Bladder Detoxification

Many books, practitioners and authorities in health care tout the benefits of liver and gall bladder detoxification or flushes. The liver, while important and essential in human nutrition and function, is not solely responsible for detoxification. The liver has almost 500 known functions, most of which are not directly related to detoxification. Therefore, in many instances liver and gall bladder flushes are overemphasized.

This in no way diminishes their essential role in the detoxification process. One of the more famous procedures for liver/gall bladder detoxification utilizes a variety of activities, culminating in the drinking of olive oil mixed with lemon juice. While favorable results have been achieved from this procedure, it is at best a most unpleasant experience. Fortunately, there are much easier and far more effective ways of accomplishing the same ends.

Colon Cleansing

Many people experience positive effects from enemas and colonics, or by adding bulk, such as psyllium husk or seed to their diet. Many also achieve good results by utilizing charcoal tablets or bentonite clay to absorb toxins in the colon.

Chelation Therapy

In general, the body is equipped to process and eliminate organic toxins occurring as byproducts of our nutritional process or food intake. At any given time, our bodies must deal with many thousands of complex organic toxins and inorganic toxins. We have no physiological mechanisms in place to break down these inorganic toxins completely.

Some toxic molecules are so large or of such a makeup that they are virtually impossible to totally expel from the system. These include many severely toxic heavy metals, such as aluminum, mercury, lead, cadmium, etc. Aluminum is implicated in Alzheimer's and other neurological conditions. Lead has a host of negative side effects, as does mercury, which has an affinity for the neurological system and bone. Cadmium is implicated in many cancers.

Chelation therapy seeks to remove these toxic substances by binding a substance to them in the bloodstream.

One compound effective against heavy metal toxicity is calcium disodium EDTA (Ethylenediaminetetraacetic acid). This compound is routinely used in chelation therapy. EDTA can bind with some of these heavy metals to facilitate excretion from the body. As a bonus, EDTA can also bind with fat and calcium molecules in the bloodstream and is believed to be effective in combating hardening of the arteries and cholesterol buildup in the bloodstream. This ability makes chelation therapy using EDTA an effective treatment for circulatory problems and cardiovascular conditions.

However, EDTA will also bind with minerals in the body; therefore, mineral replacement is highly recommended. The most traditional procedure requires administration of an IV in the doctor's office one to two times weekly. Within a day or two, a follow-up IV is required for the replacement of minerals.

EDTA can also be administered orally, although because of the route it must take (through the stomach), it is felt to be less effective than IV administration. Another option, which has great promise, is administration via a suppository form of EDTA called KelaminHM". Studies indicate that KelaminHM" is as effective, if not more effective, than intravenous chelation therapy.

While the evidence clearly concludes that both are excellent forms of chelation therapy, there are two major differences between IV chelation therapy and KelaminHM. One is the cost. Intravenous chelation can cost anywhere from $1,000 to $1,500 for a series of ten treatments. The same amount of EDTA from KelaminHM, including the minerals, is approximately $350.

Intravenous chelation therapy per round of treatment is administered much faster. The EDTA is delivered over a series of ten IVs per round. In KelaminHM, the same amount of chelation is administered with 30 suppositories. In a condition where one needs extremely fast results at high levels of EDTA, the IV route may be more beneficial.

Because chelation only extracts heavy metal toxins from the bloodstream, and those toxins tend to accumulate in nerves and bone, extracting them completely may be a long process. Under those circumstances, it may be that a slower approach using the suppositories will yield greater results.

With chelation's proven effectiveness and the mounting research concerning the negative effects of these toxic substances upon human health, chelation therapy, whether by IV or KelaminHM, should be an essential component in any serious detoxification regimen.

Raw Foods

Consider a meal of raw vegetables or fruits once a day. The unprocessed, uncooked nature of the food will energize your body's own natural detoxification mechanisms. Certain factors in nutrition are known to provide antioxidant properties, which neutralize many toxic compounds that produce negative side effects. These antioxidant properties are all found in raw fruits and vegetables.

This is a partial list of general detoxification methods available today. All such programs are best evaluated by taking a personal inventory of your symptoms and conditions and reevaluating after a trial period of your program of choice.

Chapter 14
Other Alternative Therapies

"It is reasonable to expect the doctor to recognize that science may not have all the answers to problems of health and healing."

– Norman Cousins

This book has covered a wide variety of healing modalities. This chapter will focus on one of the less commonly known healing therapies: Protomorphogen (PMG) Therapy

Protomorphogen Therapy

The late 19th and early 20th centuries enjoyed something of a renaissance in natural healing. Drs. Weston Price, Francis Pottenger and Royal Lee were some of the major developers of concepts in nutritional therapies that have endured to this day. Dr. Lee's work has proven to be instrumental in understanding how the immune system works.

Through Dr. Lee's dedication to understanding the powers of nutritional healing, he developed the theory that specific protein chains can encourage certain healing processes in the body. Dr. Lee had to invent the machinery capable of extracting the intact DNA chains without destroying them. Once he perfected his extraction technique, Dr. Lee extracted intact DNA from the nucleus of certain animal tissues. His first extract was of heart tissue that resulted in a product called Cardiotrophin PMG. From this beginning, Dr. Lee went on to develop a line of therapeutic agents he called "protomorphogens" (PMGs).

Dr. Lee concluded that many protomorphogens could be found and utilized in healing as long as they are extracted in their intact and pure form. Therefore, when a person has a problem related to a specific organ function, ingestion of the appropriate protomorphogen made from that particular gland or organ may be useful in facilitating that individual's self-healing and self-regenerating capacity. Practitioners and patients utilizing these products have often reported favorable results for more than 75 years. Protomorphogens are available only through licensed healthcare professionals. PMGs are usually in tablet form and are taken orally as a nutritional supplement. The only company to offer these supplements is Standard Process, Inc., which has carried on Dr. Lee's work.

Protomorphology and Autoimmune Dysfunction

Dr. Lee also theorized decades ago that one of the major causes of human ailments is autoimmune dysfunction. He theorized that the same protomorphogens used to revitalize organs and tissues could be utilized to identify and treat autoimmune conditions. The physiology demonstrating the benefits of Dr. Lee's theories was not available for over 50 years. As scientific research uncovers some of the underlying mechanisms, there may be more explanations as to why Dr. Lee's theories and protocols are often effective and lend credence to his research conclusions.

In the early days of genetics, it was believed that when a cell divides, it makes an absolute perfect replica of itself. It was later discovered that cellular replication in humans may not be as perfect as we had once thought. Factors such as stress, inadequate nutrition, or a host of unidentified factors can affect cell replication. As the body is producing its replacement cells, it will place a high priority on getting the job done in a timely fashion, even if this means slight imperfections are produced. The new cell might have imperfections that alter that cell's function, or it could simply be a "cosmetic" imperfection on the outside surface of the cell. This unintended imperfection is believed to create the autoimmune dysfunction.

The immune system identifies the differences between foreign invaders and resident cells by touch. In other words, the immune cells touch the cellular membrane of everything that they encounter and compare that touch to the body's unique blueprint. By this process of recognition, the immune system deciphers between cells that belong and those that don't.

Only cells identified as foreign invaders trigger an immune response. Healthy resident cells are ignored. However, if an organ is sick, ailing, malnourished or stressed, it may not have had all the resources needed to reproduce perfect cellular membranes. Then, the immune system may identify the sick organ as familiar but not quite part of its own body. The sick organ may then have an immune response, similar to a reaction to a cold, flu or an infected cut. Or, the immune system could mount a response against the healthy organ to help "clean up" the debris it discovered through its touch identification process. The immune system response wouldn't be a full-scale attack on the sick organ. It would enact a partial immune response to rid the body of the defective materials. The immune response creates added stress to the already ailing organ or tissue.

A body being subtly attacked by its own immune system rarely presents in a full-blown illness. In cases like these, complaints are often vague, unidentifiable or generalized. Frequently and regrettably, an overactive immune system is blamed. Patients are then given immune suppressors or inhibitors, which do nothing to correct the underlying problem. Too often, the immune system is blamed for these kinds of problems when it's just doing its intended job.

Using PMGs in Subclinical Autoimmune Dysfunction

Realizing the potential value of PMGs in the treatment of subclinical autoimmune dysfunction, Dr. Lee formulated a specific protocol to identify and treat such circumstances. His protocol includes taking PMGs on an empty stomach to facilitate the PMG introduction into the body.

The specific DNA chains contained in the protomorphogen must be absorbed into the bloodstream intact without breaking down in the digestive system. By taking these products on an empty stomach, the digestive response isn't initiated. Thus, the supplements are transported to the gut intact, are absorbed into the bloodstream, and then migrate to the organ without being altered.

The diagnostic test for autoimmune dysfunction is to observe the patient's response to the ingestion of the protomorphogen. If an individual is suffering from some degree of subclinical autoimmune dysfunction, the PMGs will cause one of three possible responses. Upon ingestion of PMGs, the person with an autoimmune dysfunction will either: 1) tend to feel better; 2) tend to feel worse; or 3) have a delayed response. On those rare occasions when the response is delayed significantly, the person may require a long-term administration of PMGs to elicit the healing response. However, most of the time, an observable response will manifest within a few days to a week.

The ideal response is for the individual consuming the proper PMG to feel better. Should this occur, the strategy is to keep taking the protomorphogen. The current theory is that if the patient feels better from taking a protomorphogen, it's because the PMG in the gut was found by the immune system cells circulating in the bloodstream, seeking out the target malformed cells. Since the protomorphogen resembles the ailing organ or gland, some of the immune response that has been attempting to clean up the debris of the ailing organ will be distracted by the PMG in the gut. By diverting the immune response, the weakened organ or tissue is less stressed. The patient simply feels better.

Depending on the circumstances, the patient and physician may also decide to feed the ailing organ with specific nutrition to assist in the rebuilding of the organ, assuring ultimate recovery. This strategy represents a twofold approach: 1) de-stressing the organ by utilizing the

PMG between meals; and 2) rebuilding the organ by taking other nutritional complexes with meals. For example, with adrenal dysfunction, Drenatrophin PMG is taken between meals while Drenamin is taken with meals.

The other response to the therapeutic trial of a PMG is when the patient feels worse. Luckily, this effect is typically limited to five to ten minutes in length; therefore, the patient does not need to experience prolonged discomfort to identify the autoimmune condition. The practitioner should be aware, however, that in some extreme cases or sensitive individuals, more prolonged exacerbations are possible. This should not present a deterrent to this form of therapy, but alert one to the need for developing an individualized dosage regimen.

Some people may feel mood changes or fatigue. Others may feel the classic histamine response, sort of like an allergy. Others may experience an exacerbation of whatever symptoms have been their main concern. Sometimes these responses aren't noticeable until the third day of the protomorphogen trial.

If adverse effects from the ingestion of protomorphogens is experienced, two major strategies can be implemented.

It's often recommended that patients simply "tough out" the negative response to the protomorphogen ingestion. This isn't harmful and over time is therapeutic. The body will simply become strong enough that the histamine response is not an issue.

There is a much simpler solution. The "negative" response to the ingestion of a protomorphogen is because the liver is suddenly responsible for breaking down more of the toxic byproducts caused by the protomorphogen. Histamines are released and can make the patient feel bad. This "reaction" can be alleviated quite simply by the ingestion of a product containing Yakitron, which facilitates certain functions of the liver. It allows this organ to break down the histamine reactions more efficiently, therefore alleviating the symptoms. Furthermore, when an extreme autoimmune dysfunction is identified and treated with PMG therapy, the target organ may be supplemented at mealtime by the appropriate nutritional complexes.

Identification of Specific Autoimmune Dysfunction

The identification of the appropriate target organ in autoimmune dysfunction is only occasionally obvious. It is usually a bit mysterious. The function of various organs and glands are interrelated and interdependent in the normal human physiological system. Therefore, almost any dysfunction can cause almost any symptom. The best physicians trained in the study of protomorphology can often narrow down a patient's dysfunction to three to five systems. This still requires a "trial and error" process to identify the major dysfunctional system.

Protomorphology can be an amazing and effective way of treating symptoms of disease and/or promoting health or wellbeing.

Chapter 15

Conclusion

*"You cannot swim for new horizons until you have
courage to lose sight of the shore."*
                                   – William Faulkner

Why do people get sick? The reasons are incredibly varied and include nutritional, mental, emotional, energetic and, of course, structural components. One of the main intentions of this book is to examine how structural components influence health and healing of the human condition.

Mitchell Waller DC was an exceptional student of mine. After completing a four-year undergraduate degree, a Doctor of Chiropractic must pursue a 10-semester postgraduate course of study. Mitch elected to go even further and entered a master's degree program in Biomechanics. No small accomplishment!

Part of the post-doctorate program was to devise and execute a project. Dr. Waller designed a project that was truly a stroke of genius, inner guidance or inspiration. He did a series of very simple experiments. He asked a group of individuals to go kick a soccer ball. With very few exceptions those individuals would innately kick a ball with the right foot, with only one exception. Trained dancers who are schooled in symmetry for many years did not always exhibit this nearly exclusive pattern of right dominance in this activity.

Another experiment was to measure the force exerted as individuals jumped from an 18-inch platform onto a plate that would measure the force of impact and compare the pressure upon landing of the right and left legs. Almost all tested favored the left side of the body to absorb more impact than the right. This result was unfailingly consistent in the course of this experiment.

The conclusion was that there is some central nervous system, hardwiring mechanism that prefers right dominance for certain activities and left dominance for other activities. This sets the stage for certain biomechanical imbalances.

Additional research exploring the causes of structural imbalance are being conducted by Dr. Dennis Ennis at Logan College of Chiropractic, in association with the St. Louis University School of Medicine. Dr. Ennis, initially in conjunction with the Biomechanics Department of the University of Missouri Columbia, performed castings of the sacroiliac joints of several cadavers. The castings were then submitted for measurements to determine the exact contours and architecture of this joint.

The findings were that in every single individual tested, the sacroiliac joint was not symmetrical. In other words, the design and contours were different from right to left. They were also found to differ from person to person.

Overall this information demonstrates that we are not designed in perfect symmetry from right to left. The sacroiliac joint is the base of the human tower, our center of gravity. Any minute imbalance in the sacroiliac joint produces a pattern of distortion, stressing the entire spinal column, and in turn, distorting the cranial structure and cerebral spinal fluid pump mechanism.

Imagine a television tower with a wobbly base. Now place that tower on a floating platform on the ocean. The top would be wildly swaying in all directions, reacting to every tiny motion of the water's surface. This is exactly the sort of constantly changing forces that the human spine and cranium must navigate with our every movement. The brain, nervous system and cranium are charged with this massive and constant duty.

In an investigational study, yet to be published, I performed photographic analysis of 15 skulls of various mammals and 10 human skulls. In this study it is apparent that all the other-than-human animals were consistently symmetrical, while all the human skulls were consistently asymmetrical, and I postulated that the measured cranial distortions ultimately result from adaption to pelvic subluxations.

From these investigations, one can assert the possibility that humans suffer from so much low back pain and cranial issues because we are inherently built to be asymmetrical and, therefore, imbalanced. To complicate matters further, our upright stature accentuates these minute differences.

My skull studies were the subject of a presentation at the request of the Brazilian Chiropractic College in São Paulo, Brazil. This information was first presented in 2012 at the Universidade Anhembi Morumbi (UAM)

While all this research is not yet published in the scientific journals, it does suggest a plausible rationale for what is considered an epidemic of low back pain in the United States. What we do know is that the traditional medical treatments for low back pain, as well as acute and chronic brain dysfunction, have demonstrated themselves to be relatively unsuccessful for the last half a century. Of course, they do not take into consideration the De Jarnette Cranial Syndrome (DCS), or his Category II subluxation complex.

These investigations also underscore a tenant Dr. De Jarnette and others have repeatedly championed, i.e., that these distortion patterns are very prominent and are most easily corrected in the younger person. Children and even infants could benefit greatly by having a qualified craniopath evaluate and treat for these dysfunctions at an early age. This could indeed prevent many structural issues throughout the rest of their lives.

The body of information contained herein represents a fraction of the tip of the iceberg with respect to the total amount of investigations dedicated to understanding and treating health issues, including brain dysfunction. There are many powerful, effective interventions that are sorely underutilized because they are not recognized or understood by organized medicine. This does not make them less essential or potent, just misunderstood. The least recognized aspect is probably the paramount relationship between structure and function in health and healing. These concepts have been championed over a century by great medical thinkers but have yet to be embraced on a widespread scale. Even Thomas Edison demonstrated an understanding as evidenced by his famous quote,

"The doctor of the future will give no medicine but will interest his patients in the care of the human frame, in diet and in the cause and prevention of disease."

What is the importance of this body of information? To paraphrase: pelvic imbalance produces cranial distortion and subluxations in the human being. Cranial subluxations alter cerebral spinal fluid pressures and flow patterns in the cranium. These changes, however small, produce neurological imbalances, and therefore, impede the brain's ability to execute healing functions throughout the entire body.

Only when we start looking outside the mainstream medical box will we begin to see the bigger picture of health and disease.

This book illustrates just a few of the many lives that are being impacted, if not saved, by applying these nontraditional strategies.

Chiropractic physicians in the United States are licensed as primary health care professionals, i.e., trained and licensed to diagnose disease. However, chiropractors are not licensed to prescribe medications or perform surgeries. Part of the responsibility of chiropractors is also to identify medical conditions and refer patients to a medical doctor (MD) or doctor of osteopathy (DO), if needed.

Because of these legalities, the chiropractor has a greater responsibility than does the traditional medical doctor. The other professions aren't trained in the diagnosis and identification of the Category II subluxation complex. Therefore, they are not required to refer patients to chiropractors, if the patient requires that specialty.

Chiropractic physicians help people daily to resolve conditions that have confounded medical doctors and do so at a fraction of the cost. Since its inception in 1895, chiropractic has grown to become the largest natural healthcare profession in the world. Chiropractic colleges have been established, not only in the U.S., but internationally, and the profession is continually growing to meet the needs of the worldwide population.

Surprisingly, chiropractic has not become more popular in the United States, the country where it originated. While there's greater acceptance of chiropractic in general, the number of people who seek chiropractic care is proportionately about the same as it was when I received my doctorate degree in 1978. Why is that the case?

There is no simple answer to this question. Sometimes it is fear; however, chiropractic has been proven by numerous studies to be extremely safe. This fact is reflected in the price of malpractice insurance, e.g. mine is a mere fraction of that of my medical counterparts.

Another factor may be the numerous misunderstandings about chiropractic in general. As you have read in the case studies contained in this book, many conditions, some even life threatening, were helped significantly by these procedures. Sadly, the concept of the subluxation is poorly understood and not generally accepted by mainstream healthcare. There is overwhelming evidence of its efficacy in scientific literature. Clinical successes are seen and experienced in offices worldwide daily. Yet prejudice and misunderstanding remain powerful forces in human behavior.

These issues are escalated further when it comes to the discipline of Chiropractic Craniopathy. This is a specialty that is practiced by a tiny fraction of practicing chiropractors today. Few certified Chiropractic Craniopaths exist worldwide. Even fewer fully understand and properly diagnose the De Jarnette Cranial Syndrome (DCS) and apply the total Integrated Sutural Protocol (ISP).

So how does Sacro Occipital Technic (SOT), SOT Chiropractic Craniopathy, the De Jarnette Cranial Syndrome and the Integrated Sutural Protocol fit into the traditional medical healthcare system? These disciplines are highly specialized subsets of the entire healthcare complex. There should be far more qualified and capable practitioners; however, awareness of these specialties is limited in the public, as well as in the whole of the medical profession.

Which is why personal responsibility and individual choice become so essential. Patients, their caretakers and loved ones need to be educated and take personal responsibility. This book is designed to assist in that educational process for all. The next step is up to you.

Things You Can Do

There is a great need for research to better understand the missing links of brain dysfunction and degeneration. Additionally, education of qualified practitioners is also the essence. Tax-deductible contributions for research and education can be made through the Sacro Occipital Research Society International, Inc. www.SORSI.com

Your donations of any amount contribute to the continued efforts of SORSI and her international organizations to further understand the undiscovered functions of the human cranium and support doctors in their training to become proficient at these specialized technologies.

Remember Ryan who is enjoying a miraculous recovery from a devastating and life-threatening stroke? One of his amazing healing attributes was ATTITUDE. What you think and feel affects your neurology just as your neurology affects your thoughts and physiology. Never underestimate the power of the human mind. There are many great resources on this subject. Serious dedication to the teachings of any of these volumes will prove to be life changing. Here are just a few:

As a Man Thinketh by James Allen

The Power of Positive Thinking by Norman Vincent Peale

The Greatest Salesman in the World by Og Mandino

The Psychology of Winning by Denis Waitley

A growing number of authors and teachers provide valuable information and resources for self-help. The short list is by no means comprehensive.
Dr. Joseph Mercola www.mercola.com

Saving Your Brain by Dr. Kelly Miller

Why Isn't My Brain Working? By Dr. Datis Kharrazian

For more information concerning chiropractic, check out The American Chiropractic Association at www.acatoday.org and the World Federation of Chiropractic at www.wfc.org Dr. Rick Serola has developed a sacroiliac belt designed to help stabilize the human pelvis. Information concerning this device as well as some of his research can be found at www.serola.net

Sacro Occipital Research Society International, Inc. (SORSI) was founded by Dr. Major Bertrand De Jarnette in 1957 to be the custodian of his life's work. SORSI, along with her sister organizations, formed Sacro Occipital Technique Organization International (SOTO-I). Ongoing instructional programs and investigations based upon Dr. De Jarnette's inventions, 138 books and countless publications are administered by the legitimate authorized agencies worldwide. For more information concerning The Sacro Occipital Technic™ Methods of healing and a list of current practitioners see www.SORSI.com

The oldest and most trusted company producing whole food concentrates for nutritional healing is Standard Process Inc. with more information at www.StandardProcess.com

More information and resources are available through the website dedicated to this book. As new and more research and pertinent information is made available, it will be posted at www.BrainMattersTheMissingLink.com

Appendix A

Nephi Cottam DC

Nephi Cottam DC (1883-1966) published the first written descriptions of cranial adjusting in modern times, very close the same time William O. Sutherland DO also began publishing his investigations into craniopathy. Both pioneers confronted the status quo and conventional understanding to develop their experiences and discoveries with cranial adjusting. Others followed even into current times with evolving research, understanding and techniques. I'm not reproducing an exhaustive list of all that should be commemorated because I would surely miss some. There were and continue to be many dedicated practitioners and researchers.

For many years I had always heard and believed that Dr. Sutherland was the founder of modern day Craniopathy. The first information that I received to the contrary was a student of mine at Logan College of Chiropractic. Mary Harrington researched the historical aspects of craniopathy as her senior research project for which I was an advisor. Dr. Harrington was the first to alert me to the work of Dr. Nephi Cottam.

I found the following excerpt about Nephi Cottam of great interest, from "**History of Cranial Therapy**."

Nephi Cottam, D.C.

In the mid-twenties, Dr. Nephi Cottam discovered the power and effectiveness of cranial manipulation when he performed a cephalad lift on the cranial vault of a seated patient. This procedure provided immediate relief to the woman, who had been hysterically running around screaming, pulling her hair, tearing her clothes, and destroying furnishings for three days (Calvin Cottam, 1990). Eight days later he performed a similar procedure on a young woman who had not been able to sleep for three months without opiates. She had lost her eyesight and hearing and was near death. After Cottam performed a cranial release the patient lapsed into normal sleep and soon recovered (Cottam did not elaborate on how long 'soon' was). These successes impressed Cottam enough that he began to research cranial manipulative techniques on his patients and later taught his techniques to others.

Cottam's techniques were spread across the United States and Canada, then into Europe by visiting doctors who had witnessed his demonstrations. In 1929, George A. Cole, D.C., began teaching Cottam's cranial adjusting techniques throughout the United States. Cottam named his techniques 'Craniopathy' in 1932. Four years later he moved to Los Angeles. There, in 1936, he published The Story of Craniopathy and founded the Cottam School of Craniopathy. The cranial teachings of Cottam (and his two sons) profoundly influenced the chiropractic profession. Many of the legendary chiropractic practitioners were associated with cranial manipulative techniques (which could explain how they achieved the results for which they are remembered!).

In reviewing Dr. Cottam's material, he focused upon cranial bone motion and sutural functions. Dr. Sutherland emphasized the subtle motions of the Cranial Sacral Respiratory Mechanism.

Major Bertrand De Jarnette DC was a student of Sutherland and never claimed to originate Chiropractic Craniopathy. His genius was to integrate an understanding of the various perspectives of cranial manipulation into a synthesized system of analysis and correction. De Jarnette described these two mechanisms as separate but integrated parts of the whole system. Each system has a different set of tests, measures and indicators of dysfunction, as well as most effective treatment protocols. In the terminology of the Sacral Occipital Technic (SOT®) they are termed Category I and Category II. Category I refers mostly to the Cranial Sacral

Respiratory Mechanism. Category II refers to the osseous connections in the cranium comprising the sutural system. This involves the De Jarnette Cranial Syndrome (DCS).

Since Dr. Cottam appears to be the first to report the use of osseous cranial manipulation to affect the human condition. His accounting of the first adjustment utilizing Chiropractic Craniopathy is of interest and significance. This chapter is reproduced in its entirety here from the 1985 book **"Cranial and Facial Adjusting Step-By-Step"** by Calvin Cottam DC. This following reproduction on the next page is identical to the original including the artwork.

INTRODUCTION

"There are three steps in the history of a great discovery. First, its opponents say that the discoverer is crazy; later that he is saying but that his discovery is of no real importance; and last, that the discovery is important that everybody has known it right along."

-Sigmund Freud

A portion of M. Gehin's contribution has been to gather together techniques from various traditions. Although we urged M. Gehin to identify the source of each technique, he declined, believing that such attribution was impertinent and could be misleading inasmuch as the techniques were best regarded as belonging to a common heritage. [From editors preface to English version of Gehin's 1981 book, "Atlas of Manipulative Techniques for the Cranium and Face" published November, 1985. The first cranial adjustment.]

Excerpt from **Head First for Health** by Calvin Cottam,© 1952, 1980. Drawings, 1985.©

"It is seldom that you see the technical side of any healing art written up in such an entertaining style as we find in the book "**Head First for Health.**" In between the lines, there is a story that all humanity could listen to.

"Truly, our greatest amount of healing has come when we have taken care of the 'Head' first. Here is a novel way of bringing out to this fact — and the subject of healing is accomplished in a new way.

Head First for Health dealing with "Craniopathy" will tax your imagination and feed your mind with a new outlook to the healing art."

– Bernard Jensen, DC

Tim cried out, "Doc, there must be something you can do. You've been here two days and nights trying to call my wife, but she's still about the same. Look at her. She's pulling her hair out again." As a milder afterthought he added, "she's torn everything in the house, she might as well tear her hair." He picked up some rags from the floor as he said, "these used to be pretty draperies, but they are shreds now... And you know, we were pretty proud of all her belongings, but I'll bet the junkman wouldn't have any of them now that she's ripped and broken them all to pieces.

"Martha's screaming again and caring what little there is left of her dress. DOC, you've got to do something!"

The words resounded in the ears of Nephi Cottam. They hit and hollow mockery. He thought "what more can I do? I've tried everything I know. She's calm down a little.... But a little is not very much for woman who's turned in sane." His feelings of wanting to be of help for as the knocker of a bell clanging against the broken shell of the inade-quate knowledge he then had.

Tim and Martha were not their names, but the eventually happened in the middle of the 1920s.

Cottam started straightening his tie, as a hint to the husband that he planned to leave, and said, "everything that I know how to do has been done…"

Screeeeam!

Before any more can be said, Tim answered him by going to the door, turning the lock, and saying as he put the key in his pocket, "Dr.… You're going to stay here… until Martha's quiet." His strained eyes pierced Cottam's depths as he added quite happily, "look, she seems to like it because I've made you stay. She's just standing there, quiet like, and watching us… But there she goes again. Why can't Martha stop screaming and pulling at the top of her head. DOC, if she doesn't stop soon, I'm going to go mad, too."

As he spoke, an idea began performing in Cottam's brain. "Maybe she's trying to tell us something by the way she's acting. Notice as she goes by, that she yells and simultaneously grabs the top of her head and yanks her hair?"

"Does it mean anything?" Tim question.

"I've an idea, though it may sound silly…"

Nothing scratch and "nothing would sound silly to me now, Dr. period"

"A thought keeps flashing through me of what to do, but such a thing has never been done before, that I know of."

"What is it?"

"It seems to me that the head is too 'tight'; if we loose in it, she ought to calm down."

"Sounds simple enough. But how do you do it?"

"An idea is haunting me. It's as if a voice is telling me just what to do. There are sutures which are like seams where the bones join together to form the head. If they would 'give' a little and the cells of the head expand and have more ease, the pressure on the brain might be reduced."

"Do it; stop pacing the floor, and do it. There has to be a first time in anything."

"But I really don't know what will happen."

Tim looked Cottam straight in the eyes and with a searching, pleading stair replied, "whatever it is, try it. Martha's better off dead than alive this way. She couldn't be any worse. What can I do to help you?"

Something seemed to be telling Cottam just what to do and say as he said to Tim, "hold her in a chair… That straight back one from the kitchen will be fine." Tim brought Martha from the other room and put her in the chair.

"Here she is. I'll hold her like this. Okay?"

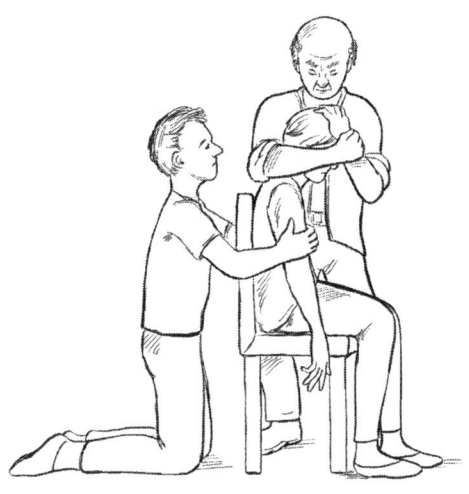

Only for use by health professionals are under their direct supervision. Copyright, 1985 Calvin Cottam, DC

It looked to Tim as though the doctor just put his hands in front and back of her head in a way that he had never seen before, and then made a strange movement with his hands. Tim showed his amazement as he exclaimed, "what was that? It sounded like all the bones in her body clicked."

But before he could expresses astonishment, Martha calmly looked at Cottam and said with a sigh of relief, "Dr.... Why didn't you do that for? The pain has gone!"

Such a quick response had them amazed. Cottam's only answer to her was, "I didn't know how!"

For a moment there was a stifling silence. Then Tim broke the unusual quiet by asking, "darling, why did you scream so and tear everything you could get your hands on? What made you act the way you did?"

Martha burst into tears as she replied, I knew I'd been acting 'crazy'. I knew all the things I was doing, but I couldn't help it. There was a pain in my head as if a hammer was pounding pins and needles into it. At first there will was just a headache, but it got so bad that I tried anything to get it to stop. When I hit my head against the wall, it would get sort of non-and feel 'better' for a while. But, the hammers just kept pounding and pounding and... Oh, now, that they stopped, let me forget it. I'm limp as a dishrag. Public get to the other room. I've got to sleep. I've just got to rest."

After Tim returned from the bedroom, where he left his wife to repose in the deep quiet of recovery, he took the key from his pocket and said, "Dr., I don't know what you did, but you must've done something. Martha's surely calm now. The change happened so suddenly I hardly know what to say."

Tim turned the key and bade farewell to the doctor.

Nephi Cottam*started home. His brain was spinning in wondering thoughts that were to change his whole life.

> *Pronounced Ne as in need, phi as in find,
> Cottam as in caught 'em.

What have I done?

"What they done?" The thought taunted him. "Why, why... Why? What made her stop raving in become sane? Could be that I really did move the bones and relieve a pressure in her head? All the books I've ever read and all I've been taught in school sets forth the idea that the bones of the skull are immovable! Had I really done anything, or had her condition run its course so that it was just a coincidence that she became calm when she did?"

Cottam turned the problem over to those two inner conflicting forces which hound and bless us in moments of decision, — let's call them "Zum" and "Zy" — the conventional versus the exploratory.

Zum

Zum is the little man within whose always willing to let the other fellow figure things out. He's filled with doubt and always willing to believe that everything worth knowing has already been discovered and accepted by "those in the know". He firmly maintains the idea that the great achievements and discoveries are brought to light only in the impressive, expensive laboratories were people have the equipment with which to "think" and find out. He is certain that everything worth knowing is already in books, and that all one has to do is look it up. To him, one who finds things out is in a far distant tower surrounded by the clouds of genius, based with the sunlight of inspiration, and unapproachable by common occurrences. He believes that in that which is popular, conventional, and in the good graces of the masses in power at the moment. He'll gladly change his ideas next week if by doing so he agrees with the majority and he can be "one of the gang."

Zy

Zy, the other self, is quite a different fellow. He also is filled with doubts, but his are of another kind. He welcomes everything that is true, even if there aren't a lot of people ready to agree with him and Pat his back in adulation. He senses that greater things are just waiting to be discovered by those who set out to find them. He remembers that there is something with in each person that enables him to find answers if his whole being is receptive to the whisperings of the infinite. He believes in universal law and order. He labels a law "true" if it always did work, if it does now, and if he expects it to very likely operate in the future when put into operation didn't use the same way.

Zy is a true optimist. He believes in cause and effect. He firmly looks forward to the fact that if you truly seek after something, you're bound to find an answer. He is a realist, for he believes that the answer might be "no" or "maybe" as well as "yes". He remembers that the outer appearance of a person, or his schooling has nothing to do with stability to tap into the knowledge of the universe. He believes that where the man lives, how much he makes, and who he knows, are of little importance to the Giver of Wisdom.

Seeing the sutures in a new way

Cottam was in his office as a Zum inside began their dual. Zum said, "all right, Cottam, down and take it easy. You've done enough for the day. Just shut your eyes and go to sleep."

Zy retorted, "listen, Zum, you be quiet. You're the one who should go to sleep. I have things to talk over with Cottam. Zy continued, Cottam, see that skull up there in yourself? Get it down and look at it. All you've done to it for years is dusted off. It's time that you saw what is really all about. Come on now, examine it. That's right. Put it over here with a light is better. Really look at it and remember what you did with Martha. See all the seams in the skull? All the bones are placed together in triangles where they join. This seems are all dovetailed in scale like. Look at the bottom of the skull. See the openings with the bones meet together? There like Windows, aren't they? When you had your hands on Martha's had and lifted up the frontal bone, see how you changed the relation of all the bones to one another? By doing that you gave were greater room in the brain and expanded the whole head."

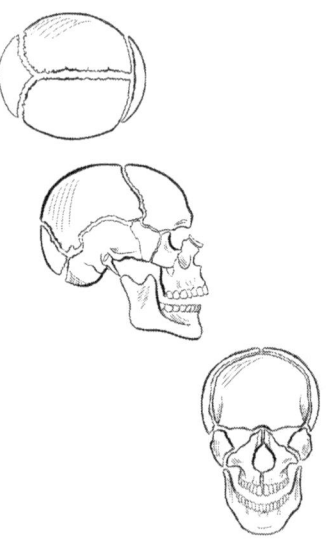

"Now just a minute," Zum chimed in. He had been waiting for a chance to break into the conversation. "Who do you think you're kidding? You looking at a skull as if it were crystal ball or something. Shake it. See how it rattles. See how brutal the bones are. Why, if you tried to move those bones you to break the skull.

Dead!

Zum, doubting his usual, seem to have a worthy point to think about until Zy set forth with both barrels.

"You've been ruling the roost long enough. It's time you were told a thing or two. You're absolutely right in what you say. The dead *skull is* brittle and does rattle and would be apt to break her crack if you try to move the bone. But all you've ever examined and thought about is a dead *skull. It* is time you realize that he living person is very different from a cadaver."

Alive!

Zum, unconvinced, vented his wrath: "listen here, just because Cottam's mother was a Swedish naturalist and was always emphasizing nature, urging him towards worthy purposes in life, you're not going to get him off on some wild tangent. Years ago he was doing all right teaching music and selling pianos until you got him interested in taking this matter of health seriously."

"And what would you have Cottam do?"

"Well… I'd never have had him become a doctor. It's all your fault he got interested in studying Chiropractic. He ought to have stayed put, instead of gallivanting all over the country learning too much. You know a little knowledge is a dangerous thing, and now he's apt to start getting some ideas of his own."

"And why shouldn't he?"

"What will people say?"

"Listen, Zum, at the school Cottam intended they had one of the largest non-medical clinics in the world. Many "miracles" were performed there. People came from all of the world to receive help."

"Well then, Zy, let him go back to school some more and read some more books."

"My dear friend, Cottam is seeking answers to the wise of health and living not yet in books. Nor are they in the fund of knowledge already discovered."

So Nephi Cottam, chiropractor, started his lifelong research of cranial adjusting which he named craniopathy — the first known person in the history of the world to proclaim that the bones of the head might have movement between one another and might be "adjusted" to influence health, and to devise a comprehensive system of technic.

Appendix B

"Technique" versus "Technic"

Throughout Dr. De Jarnette's materials, as available through the Sacro Occipital Research Society International, (SORSI), the terms "Technique" and "Technic" are utilized. Dr. De Jarnette never did or said anything without a specific and valid reason.

In 1983, Ned Heese DC, FICS wrote a memo in the SOTO Bulletin about this topic:

> Sacro Occipital Technic is just that. It is not Sacro Occipital Technique. Sacro Occipital Technic is a coined and copyrighted series of words referring to this special chiropractic procedure. There has never been a manual published covering SOT that has been spelled other than Sacro Occipital Technic...Remember, Technic. In reference to cranial, extremity and manipulative reflex, etc., we do use Technique.

Further insights and clarifications are provided by Dave Beltakis, DC:

> As I had an engineering background when I started learning SOT, the word 'technic' was a more accurate term than 'technique.' Even though they are often defined the same, technic has a professional connotation. It is a term that a PE (Professional Engineer) would use. For example: Billy Bob (down at the hardware store) would share his technique; an engineer would give you a technic. The difference? A technique may work for an individual [while] a technic works for everyone. As simplistic as this may sound, Dr. De Jarnette's use of that term signifies a very logical, methodical and technical person.

From the dictionary:

tech·nic n. 1. technics (used with a sing. or pl. verb) The theory, principles, or study of an art or a process. 2. technics (used with a pl. verb) Technical details, rules, or method

All his procedures such as category procedures, specific cranial adjustments, extremity procedures, etc. are, more accurately, techniques. Dr. De Jarnette founded SOT in 1925 and SORSI in 1929 to carry on his studies and teachings. SORSI and its authorized international organizations SOTO-Japan (Sacro Occipital Teaching Organization-Japan), SOTO-Europe, SOTO-Australasia and the developing SOTO-Brazil and SOTO-South America in Chile continue to utilize these distinctions, as per Dr. De Jarnette's implicit directives.

Appendix C

The Effects of a Pelvic Blocking Procedure Upon Muscle Strength:
A Pilot Study
Joseph F Unger Jr DC, DICS; *Chiropractic Technique*, Vol. 10, No 4,
November 1998

Abstract

Objective: to evaluate muscle strength changes due to a specific chiropractic adjusting procedure.

Design: Multiple subjects

Setting: Private office

Participants: Chiropractic patients during routine office visits

Intervention: A Category II blocking procedure was performed according to the standard Sacro Occipital Technic guidelines until all Category II indicators were eliminated.

Outcomes. Muscle strength evaluations were performed on each of eight major muscle groups bilaterally, pre-and post-treatment procedures, while the patients were still supine on the treatment table.

Results: In data from 16 subjects, 15 of the 16 muscles demonstrated a statistical difference of better than ($p= 0.02$).

Conclusion: The study demonstrates a degree of objective evidence of change produced by a chiropractic treatment procedure. It suggests a methodology that may be used for further investigations and indicates the need for further investigations into the effects of the techniques used.

This is clearly not a conclusive scientific study. There were no control subjects to evaluate the effects of not doing anything on a person. That is because this was done in my office on patients who had come to me to receive treatment. It would have been irresponsible of me to not treat them under those circumstances. However, given the limitations of this study, it did demonstrate significant changes. The study was published by peer-reviewed journal and can be found by the title:

The effects of a pelvic blocking procedure upon muscle strength:
A pilot study
Joseph F Unger Jr DC, DICS
Chiropractic Technique, Vol. 10, No 4, November 1998

It must be recognized that the treatment of the Category II and the accompanying cranial sutural complex did not make the muscle stronger. The muscle strength is determined by exercise, size, etc. Those factors all remained the same. However, theoretically, there was an improvement in the neuromuscular system's ability to express that strength. In other words, the brain has a greater capacity for sending that muscle more appropriate nerve signals so that it could perform in a stronger fashion.

This is no different from what we may see in many aspects of sports performance. One recognized aspect of performance, for example, is attitude. We know that if a person performs a certain task, such as basketball or baseball or running a race, the performance can be greatly affected by their attitude or expectation of their performance. In other words, the halftime pep talk by the coach might make that team perform differently during the second half of the game. Athletes often experience the surge of adrenaline and the picking up of their pace as they hear the cheering of the crowd when approaching the finish line.

In the above experiment, I would theorize that the strength of the muscles was not changed in the participating individuals but their bodies' ability to assess that strength and perform in a stronger manner was unblocked.

The appropriate question then becomes, "What other healing capacities were also unblocked?" If a single Category II/cranial sutural intervention can produce instant changes in muscle strength, how might a series of such treatments affect the neurological system as a whole, over weeks or months?

The healing mechanisms of the body are a dynamic system. In other words, they feed on themselves and have their own internal controls and mechanisms. If the Category II subluxation complex is negatively affecting a person's healing ability, it is not possible to predict exactly what symptoms or conditions that may produce. Conversely, once a Category II subluxation is corrected, it is equally impossible to predict the total healing effects this may have on an individual.

Appendix D

Cranial Distortion and Category II Pelvic Blocking: A Pilot Study
Joseph F. Unger, Jr., D.C., F.I.C.S., Stéphane Provencher, D.C., B.S., O. Nelson DeCamp, D.C., F.I.C.S., D.A.C.A.N.

Vertebral Subluxation Research, December 18, 2009

Abstract

Purpose: The purpose of this pilot study was to measure the possible cranial anatomical landmark by photography by addressing the pelvic torsion in adult humans.

Methods: Twenty-nine subjects were chosen at random, from the student population at Logan College of Chiropractic. A vertical line was drawn at the midline of the bridge of the nose on the nasion. A photograph of the head was taken before and after the De Jarnette Category II pelvic blocking protocol. It is theorized that measurement is from the drawn vertical line to the right and left lateral border of the head.

Results: The statistical analysis of this study demonstrates significant cranial anatomical landmark changes of 2.29mm ± 1.53 (p=0.0065) during the De Jarnette Category II pelvic blocking protocol, as compared to reverse blocking and control subjects.

Conclusions: This pilot study proposes a possible cranial motion as a consideration for further study. The TMJ, cervical spinal and musculature could also be involved in the cranial anatomical landmark changes.

Key Indexing Terms: Manipulation; Chiropractic; Cranial Distortion; SOT; Category II; Pelvic Blocking

While this is an impressive study from a laboratory perspective, it does not offer conclusive proof. Many more research studies are required to thoroughly analyze and substantiate these findings. Using these concepts and theories, chiropractic physicians have helped people experience relief from symptoms and conditions worldwide.

Full Results

Cranial Distortion and Category II Pelvic Blocking - A Pilot Study

Joseph F. Unger, Jr., D.C., F.I.C.S.1
Stéphane Provencher, D.C., B.S.1
O. Nelson DeCamp, D.C., D.I.C.S., D.A.C.A.N.1
Institution: Sacro Occipital Research Society International, Inc.

Appendix E

Craniopathy: A Comparison of Training and Certifications

Chiropractic Craniopath – a chiropractic physician must become certified in SOT, advanced SOT and Chiropractic Craniopathy totaling a minimum of 250 hours of study, as well as written and oral examinations as dictated by SOTO-International.

Cranial Osteopath – an osteopathic physician must complete 40 hours of training in cranial osteopathy.

Craniosacral Therapist – requires 25 hours of training and craniosacral therapy

Other techniques – there are variety of other cranial therapies such as Bio Cranial, Endonasal Technique and numerous others; all require training and education.

Appendix F

Trigeminal Nerve Study – The official report describing the before-and-after response to the organ reflexes treatment referenced in Chapter 3.

SITE ANALYSIS:

PRE-TREATMENT
The left CN V dermatome demonstrated normal threshold at 2000 Hz., normal threshold at 250 Hz., and **moderate hyperesthesia** threshold at 5 Hz. The right CN V dermatome demonstrated normal threshold at 2000 Hz., normal threshold at 250 Hz., and normal threshold at 5 Hz. frequencies. A right versus left side site differential of 62.5% at 250 Hz., and 78.6% at 5 Hz. frequencies represents a significant abnormality of the A-delta and C-Type fibers of the CN V dermatome.

POST TREATMENT
The left CN V dermatome demonstrated normal threshold at 2000 Hz., normal threshold at 250 Hz., and a normal threshold at 5 Hz. The right CN V dermatome demonstrated normal threshold at 2000 Hz., normal threshold at 250 Hz., and **borderline hyperesthesia** threshold at 5 Hz. frequencies. A right versus left side site differential of 42.8% at 250 Hz. frequency represents a sgnificiant abnormality of the A-delta fibers of the CN V dermatome.

DISCUSSION:

The subject in this case had an abnormally low threshold (hyperesthesia) at the 5 Hz. frequency to begin with and a significant differential at the 250 Hz. as well as the 5 Hz. frequencies, all of which implicate the left side.

It is interesting to note the change in values following the treatment. This would be of interest to follow up with on a larger sample size as it would appear there was more than just a small amount of change. Reiability is determined by value consistency of less than a ten percent error in reporting between test and retest.

Reexamination of the CN V dermatome on the post examination demonstrates values consistent with initial scores at this site. This indicates the patient to be a reliable and consistent observer of sensory threshold.

Thank you for your referral.

Charles E. Wiley, M.D.
Laboratory Director

Table of Illustrations

Cover art – Jean Lopez, Graphic Design

Illustrations – Laurie O'Keefe, Medical Illustrator

Figure 1 – human head cross-section with dura 26

Figure 2 – occipital fibers. 29

Figure 3 – cranial sacral pulley concept, lateral view. 35

Figure 4 – cranial sacral pulley concept, AP view 36

Figure 5 – cranial sacral transverse pulley system 36

Figure 6 – Category II subluxation complex distortion
pattern 52

Figure 7 – Ilium/leg length relationship 53

Figure 8 – pelvic/temporal bone torque and torsion 55

Figure 9 – Ilium/internal temporal bone. 57

Figure 10 – Ilium/external temporal bone 59

Figure 11 – temporal internal/external rotation. 60

Figure 12 – temporomandibular joint with external
temporal subluxation 61

Figure 13 – temporomandibular joint with internal
temporal subluxation 62

Figure 14 – mandibular condyle position in normal
temporal bone position. 63

Figure 15 – mandibular condyle position in the
De Jarnette Cranial Syndrome 64

Figure 16 – upper cervical distortions in the De Jarnette
Cranial Syndrome. 65

Figure 17 – cranial sacral reciprocity 66

Figure 18 – flexion/extension cranial distortion. 67

Figure 19 – cranial nerve foramina in balanced skull 72

Figure 20 – cranial nerve foramina in the De Jarnette
Cranial Syndrome. 73

Figure 21 – MRI cross-section 90

Figure 22 – cranial marking syndrome in Category II
research project. 118

Figure 23 – pelvic block placement in Category II
research project. 119

Figure 24 – pre-and post-photographs related to
the Integrated Sutural Protocols. 123

Figure 25 – split image technique of photographic
analysis. 124

Figure 26 – split image technique applied pre-and
post the Integrated Sutural Protocol 125

Figure 27 – pre-and post-photo applied to the
Integrated Sutural Protocol. 127

Table of Abbreviations

CC	Certified Craniopath
CDC	Centers for Disease Control
CSF	Cerebrospinal Fluid
CSRM	Craniosacral Respiratory Mechanism
CST	Craniosacral Therapy
DCS	De Jarnette Cranial Syndrome
DICS	Diplomate International Craniopathic Society
ED	Emergency department
FICS	Fellow International Craniopathic Society
ICS	International Craniopathic Society
ISP	Integrated Sutural Protocol
MD	Medical doctor
NFMCPA	National Fibromyalgia and Chronic Pain Association
PCS	Post-Concussive Syndrome
ROM	Range of Motion
SIJ	Sacroiliac Joint
SORSI	Sacro Occipital Research Society International, Inc.
SOT®	Sacro Occipital Technic
SOTO-I	Sacro Occipital Teaching Organization - International
TBI	Traumatic Brain Injury
TMD	Temporomandibular Dysfunction
TMJ	Temporomandibular Joint

TTH   Tension-Type Headaches

WHO   World Health Organization

Glossary

Atlas – First cervical vertebra also known as C-1 (cervical 1). This vertebra is located at the base of the skull between the occiput and the second cervical vertebra.

Axis – Second cervical also known as C-2.

Category I (Cat I) – Dr. M. B. De Jarnette's term for the structural, functional and neurological mechanisms in the human body responsible for the production and distribution of cerebral spinal fluid (CSF) and the healing factors contained therein. The pelvis (hips and sacrum), cranial bones, spinal vertebrae, organs, dura mater and all its connections are included in this mechanism. The SOT® Methods embodies specific, targeted diagnostic tests and treatment protocols used by a Chiropractic Physician to treat subluxations of the Category I system.

Category II (Cat II) – Dr. M. B. De Jarnette's term for the structural, functional and neurological mechanisms in the human body responsible for the weightbearing capacity of the human body. The Cat II system is comprised of cranial, spinal, pelvic and all other components that take part in navigating the forces of gravity both structurally and neurologically. The SOT® Methods embodies specific, targeted diagnostic tests and treatment protocols used by a Chiropractic Physician to treat subluxations of the Category II system.

Category III (Cat III) – Dr. M. B. De Jarnette's term for the structural, functional and neurological mechanisms in the human body involving the connective tissues such as ligaments, tendons and discs of the spine. In the cranium, the most involved structure includes the parietal bones and their dural attachments. The SOT® Methods embodies specific, targeted diagnostic tests and treatment protocols used by a Chiropractic Physician to treat subluxations of the Category III system.

Certified Craniopath (CC) – A level of professional certification achieved by a Chiropractic Physician through SORSI or one of its official international sister organizations (SOTO-I). The Certified Chiropractic Craniopath is a licensed physician who has a minimum of 250 hours of post doctorate training with at least 5 years of clinical experience and successfully passed a battery of written and oral examinations.

Chiropractic – The philosophy, art and science of health care by removing blockages to the natural, innate healing mechanisms.

Chiropractic Adjustment – The chiropractic treatment designed to analyze and reduce neurological interference to the healing process produced by the chiropractic subluxation.

Chiropractic Subluxation – Structural, functional and/or neurological dysfunctions producing interference to the body's natural healing mechanisms. A medical "luxation" is defined as a gross misalignment of adjacent structures in the body. A "subluxation" is a smaller disturbance and can be an abnormality of motion, alignment, neurologic function and/or other factors. Chiropractic subluxations are often not always identifiable by traditional medical testing such as x-ray and are diagnosed by Chiropractic Physicians.

Chiropractic Craniopathy – The philosophy, art and science of treating cranium, structurally and functionally, as performed by Chiropractic Physicians. While closely related to other treatment modalities, such as Cranio Sacral Therapy (CST), Chiropractic Craniopathy utilizes additional interventions.

Cranial adjustment – The application of a therapeutic procedure addressing a cranial dysfunction.

Cranial Osteopathy – Cranial Sacral Therapy (CST) performed by an Osteopath with an additional 40 hours of training.

Cranial Sacral Respiratory Mechanism (CSRM) – The structures and mechanisms of the body producing and distributing cerebral spinal fluid (CSF).

Cranial Sacral Therapy (CST) – A system of balancing the Cranial Sacral Respiratory Mechanism as described by Dr. W. G. Sutherland

and developed by Dr. John Upledger. CST can be performed by anyone willing to take the training.

Cranial subluxation – A chiropractic subluxation of the cranial portion of the cranial sacral respiratory mechanism (CSRM).

Cerebral Spinal Fluid (CSF) – The liquid that bathes and nourishes the nerve cells of the central nervous system. Dr. M. B. De Jarnette, through his lifetime of research, concluded that CSF pressure, flow and proper distribution are essential factors in the innate healing process. CSF can be negatively impacted by a variety of chiropractic subluxations as described by the Sacro Occipital Technic™ Methods of Chiropractic and Chiropractic Craniopathy.

De Jarnette Cranial Syndrome (DCS) – A cranial subluxation of the sutural system as uniquely defined by Dr. M. B. De Jarnette. DCS involves the entire Category II subluxation complex including the pelvis, spine and cranium and requires the full Integrated Sutural Protocol (ISP) for optimum resolution. DCS involves the entire cranial sutural system and is distinguished from specific sutural adjustments that may be performed as part of Chiropractic Craniopathy.

Diplomat of the International Craniopathic Society (DICS) – A certification level through the International Craniopathic Society (ICS) achieved by a Chiropractic Physician having obtained the level of Certified Craniopath (CC) and then produced research accepted by the International Craniopathic Society. Authorized certifications are only issued through SORSI and SORSI–recognized SOTO-I members.

Diffuse Axonal Injury (DAI) – A type of traumatic injury resulting in irreparable damage to neurons in the brain. DAI can be mild to severe even resulting in death.

Doctor of Chiropractic (DC) – A physician graduating from a recognized chiropractic college. After premedical studies and receiving a DC degree, the chiropractic physician must pass national examinations and meet individual state requirements to obtain a license to practice.

Dura (Dura Mater) – Literally translated as "tough mother" the dura forms a sac around the brain and continues as a tube extending to the sacrum. The dura encloses the central nervous system, brain and spine, contains the cerebral spinal fluid providing nourishment, waste removal and cushion from trauma.

Fellow of the International Craniopathic Society (FICS) – A certification level achieved by the chiropractic physician who meets the requirements following the DICS status including published research in a SORSI-approved, peer-reviewed journal.

Ilia – The anatomical term for the two hip bones. One ilium is located on either side of the sacrum.

Ilium – One of the ilia. The singular form of ilia.

Integrated Sutural Protocol™ (ISP) – An integrated approach to Dr. M. B. De Jarnette's Cat II cranial sutural procedure incorporating additional procedures, as needed. The basic techniques and protocols designed by Dr. De Jarnette are preserved with inclusion of more recent discoveries in Chiropractic Craniopathy.

International Craniopathic Society (ICS) – Founded in 1984 by Dr. M. B. De Jarnette as the certifying body in Chiropractic Craniopathy still maintained through SORSI and her international sister organizations.

Neuron – A single nerve cell.

Occiput – The base bone of the skull attaching the rest of the skull to spine at the first cervical vertebra (C-1). This bone covers the occipital lobe of the brain. The occiput had a direct and reciprocal relationship to the sacrum.

Parietal – The cranial bones (2) on the sides of the head. The parietal bones cover the parietal lobes of the brain.

Pelvis – The area of the body made up by the sacrum and the two iliac bones. The pelvis is the gravitational foundation of the spine and body and is intimately related to the cranium, structurally and functionally.

Post Concussive Syndrome (PCS) – Symptoms occurring from a head injury. Most traditional therapies use methods to counteract resulting symptoms (i.e. memory exercises for memory loss). Chiropractic Craniopathy may be needed to correct the cranial subluxations resulting from the impact.

Primary Respiratory Mechanism (PRI) – The pumping action of the cranial sacral respiratory mechanism usually described as 6-12 cycles per minute. This motion occurs throughout the entire body and persists irrespective of the lung/breathing mechanism. This motion is called the cranial respiratory impulse (CRI) and is thought to be a constant, birth to death.

Sacral – Referring to the sacrum, the center bone of the pelvis.

Sacro – A term also referring to the sacrum

Sacro Occipital Technic™ (SOT®) Methods – The system of healing researched and developed by Dr. Major Bertrand De Jarnette. SOT includes evaluation and treatment of the major systems of the body's healing mechanisms, organs, structure, neurology, etc.

Sacro Occipital Research Society International, Inc. (SORSI) – The organization originally founded by Dr. De Jarnette in 1929 to carry one his teachings, research and certifications in Sacro Occipital Technic™ Methods of Chiropractic and Chiropractic Craniopathy. SORSI is the sole license holder of the rights to all of Dr. De Jarnette's teachings and writings.

Sacro Occipital Teaching Organization-International (SOTO-I) – The international body disseminating De Jarnette's works, conducting instruction to chiropractic physicians and providing certification examinations.

Sacroiliac joint (SIJ) – The junction between the sacrum and the ilia in the pelvis.

Subluxation – Technically, a misalignment that is smaller than a full luxation.

Suture – Joints in the cranium where 2 or more cranial bones meet. The cranial sutural system is the primary structure affected by the category II subluxation complex and the resulting De Jarnette Cranial Syndrome (DCS). Treatment of the full sutural system is achieved through the Integrated Sutural Protocols (ISP).

Temporal – The bones of the cranium making up the sides of the head. The ear canals and the socket for the jaw bone are found in the temporal bones. There is a direct and reciprocal connection of the hip bones (ilia) to the temporals. Subluxations of the temporal bones are often implicated in temporomandibular dysfunction and can be caused by subluxations of the pelvis.

Temporal mandibular dysfunction (TMD) – Problems with the temporomandibular joint (TMJ) that may include symptoms such as pain, clicking/popping, loss of opening/closing, etc.

Temporal mandibular joint (TMJ) – The joint in the temporal bone of the cranium that provides the attachment for the jaw bone (mandible).

Traumatic Brain Injury (TBI) – An injury involving negative effects to the brain.

Ventricles – The central part of the brain where cerebrospinal fluid (CSF) is made. Dura (Dura Mater) – Literally translated as "tough mother" the dura forms a sac around the brain and continues as a tube extending to the sacrum. The dura encloses the central nervous system, brain and spine, contains the cerebral spinal fluid providing nourishment, waste removal and cushion from trauma.

Bibliography of Research Studies in Craniopathy

Adams T, Heisey RS, Smith MC, Briner, BJ. Parietal bone mobility in the anesthetized cat. J Am Osteopath Assoc. 1992; 92:599-621.

Baker E. Alteration in width of maxillary arch and its relation to sutural movement of cranial bones. J Am Osteopath Assoc. 1970; 70:559-67.

Berkinblit MB, Deliagina TG, Orlovskii GN, Feldman AG: Activity of propriospinal neurons in cats during the scratch reflex. Neirofiziologiia 1977, 9:504-11.

Blum CL, Curl DD. The relationship between sacro-occipital technique and sphenobasilar balance, Part one: The key continuities. Chiropr Technique. 1998; 10: 95-100.

Breig A. Adverse mechanical tension in the central nervous system. New York, NY: John Wiley & Sons. 1978; p.11-53.

Buddingh CC & Zusman GS. Sphenomaxillary Craniopathy. Nebraska; 1987.

Byron CD, Borke J, Yu J, Pashley D, Wingard CJ, Hamrick M. Effets of increased muscle mass on mouse sagittal suture morphology and mechanics. The Anatomical Record. 2004; 279A (1): 676-684.

Centers for Disease Control and Prevention (CDC), National Center for Injury Prevention and Control. Guide to Writing about Traumatic Brain Injury in News and Social Media. Atlanta (GA): Centers for Disease Control and Prevention; 2015.

Chaitow L. Cranial Manipulation Theory and Practice. 2nd Edition 2005, Elsevier Ltd.

De Jarnette MB. The history of Sacro Occipital Technic. Nebraska: M. B. De Jarnette; 1958. p. 23.

De Jarnette, MB. Cranial Techniques participant guide. Kansas; 1979.

De Jarnette MB. Sacro Occipital Technic. Nebraska: M. B. De Jarnette; 1984.

De Jarnette, MB. Sacro occipital technic participant guide. Kansas; 1984.

Denton DG. Craniopathy and dentistry. California: David Denton; 1979.

Dermaut LR and Beerden L. The effects of Class II elastic force on a dry skull measured by holographic interferometry. Am J Orthod. 1981; 79:296-304.

Dutton RC, Carstens MI, Antognini JF, Carstens E: Long ascending propriospinal projections from lumbosacral to upper cervical spinal cord in the rat. Brain Res 2006, 1119:76-85.

Frymann V. A study of rhythmic motions of the living cranium Journal of the American Osteopathic Association. 1971; 70: 928-945.

Frymann V. The core-link and the three diaphragms. Academy Applied Osteopathy. 1968; 13-19. 45a.

Gray H. Gray's anatomy. Pennsylvania; 1973.

Greenman P. Roentgen findings in the craniosacral mechanism. Journal of the American Osteopathic Association. 1970; 70(1): 1-12.

Grottel K, Krutki P, Mrowczynski W. Triple projections of neurons located in S1 and S2 segments of the cat spinal cord to C6 segment, the cerebellum and the reticular formation. Exp Physiol. 1998;83(6):737-746.

Heifetz MD, Weiss M. Detextion of skull expansion with increase intracranial pressure. J Neurosurgery. 1981; 55(5): 811-812.

Heisey S, Adams T. Role of cranial bone mobility in cranial compliance. Neurosurgery. 1993; 33(5): 869-877.

Henderson JH, Longaker MT, Carter DR. Sutural bone reposition rate and strain magnitude during cranial development. Bon. 2004; 34: 271-280.

Hubbard RP, Melvin JW, Barodawala IT. Flexure of cranial sutures. J Biomech. 1971; 4(6):491-496.

Jaslow CR. Mechanical properties of cranial sutures. Journal of Biomechanics. 1990; 4: 313-321.

Kokick VG. Age changes in the human frontozygomatic suture from 20 to 95 years. Am J Orthod. 1976; 69(4): 411-430.

Kostopoulos D, Keramide G. Changes in magnitude of relative elongation of falx cerebri during application of external forces on frontal bone of embalmed cadaver. Journal of Craniomandibular Practice. 1992. January.

Kragt G., Ten Bosch JJ, Borsboom PCF. Measurement of bone displacement in a macerated human skull induced by orthodontic forces: a holographic study. J Biomechanics. 1979; 12:905-910.

Kraus SL. TMJ disorders: management of the craniomandibular complex. New York: Churchill Livingstone; 1988.

Lemaire JJ: Slow pressure waves during intracranial hypertension. 1997, 16:394-8.

Lewandoski M, Drasky E et al. Kinematic system demonstrates cranial bone movement about the cranial sutures. Journal of the American Osteopathic Association. 1996; 96(9): 551.

Libin B. Occlusal changes related to cranial bone mobility. International Journal of Orthodontic. 1982; 20(1): 13-19.

Liinamaa TL, Keane J, Richmond FJ. Distribution of motor neurons supplying feline neck muscles taking origin from the shoulder girdle. J Comp Neurol. 1997; 377(2):298-312.

Lloyd D. Mediation of Descending Long Spinal Reflex Activity. Lab Rockefeller Inst Med Res NY. 1942; July 9:435-458.

Magoun, H. Osteopathy in the Cranial Field. 1976; Journal Publishing co. Kirksville MO.

McLaughling E, Zhang Y, Pashley D, et al. The load displacement characteristics of neonatal rat cranial sutures. Cleft Palate Cranifac J. 2000; 37: 590-595.

Michael DK, Retzlaf EW. A preliminary study of cranial bone movement in the squirrel monkey. J Am Osteopath Assoc. 1975; 74:866-9.

Miller KE, Douglas VD, Richards AB, Chandler MJ, Foreman RD. Propriospinal neurons in the C1-C2 spinal segments project to the L5-S-1 segments of the rat spinal cord. Brain Res Bull. 1998;47(1):43-7.

Mitchell FL, Jr. Voluntary and involuntary respiration and the craniosacral mechanism. Osteopathic Annals. 1977; 5: 52-9.

Moskalenko Y, Kravchenko T, Gaidan B et al. Periodic mobility of cranial bones in humans. Human Physiology. 1999; 25: 51-58.

Myer R. Measurement of small rhythmic motion around the human cranium in vivo. J Aus Ost Assn. 1998.

National Fibromyalgia and Chronic Pain Association (NFMCPA), What is Fibromyalgia? http://www.fmcpaware.org/fibromyalgia/about-fm.html.

Oleski S, Smith G, Crow W. Radiographic evidence of cranial bone mobility. Cranio: Journal of Craniomandibular Practice. 2002; 20:34-43.

Olge RC, Tholpady SS, McGynn KA, Olge RA. Regulation of cranial suture morphogenesis. Cells Tissues Organs. 2004; 176 (1-3): 54-66.

Page-Echols W, Etzlaff E, Mitchell F Jr. Respiratory kinematics of ribs and sacrum: natural history and physical diagnosis interrater reliability. JAOA. 1982; 82:112.

Panjabi MM. The stabilizing system of the spine. Part I. Function, dysfunction, adaptation, and enhancement. J of Spinal Disorders. 1992; 5:383-389.

Pavlin D., Vukicevic D. Mechanical reactions of facial skeleton to maxillary expansion determined by laser holography. Am J Orthod. 1984; 85:498-507.

Pick MG. A preliminary single case magnetic resonance imaging investigation into maxillary frontal-parietal manipulation and its short-term effect upon the intercranial structures of an adult human brain. J of Manip and Physio Therapeutics. 1994; 17:168-173.

Pitlyk PJ, Piantanida TP, Ploeger DW. Noninvasive intracranial pressure monitoring. Neurosurgery. 1985; 17(4): 581-584.

Pritchard JJ, Scott JH, Girgis FG. The structure and development of cranial and facial sutures. J Anat. 1956; 90:73-85.

Retzlaff E, Mitchell F Jr, Upledger J. Aging of cranial suture in humans. Anatomy Records. 1979; 193: 663.

Rogers J, Witt P, Gross M, Hacke J, Genova P. Simultaneous palpation of the craniosacral rate at the head and feet: intrarater and interrater reliability and rate comparisons. Phys Ther. 1998; 78: 1175-85.

Schotland JL, Tresch MC. Segmental and propriospinal projection systems of frog lumbar interneurons. Exp Brain Res. 1997;116:283-98.

Sears TA. Investigation on respiratory motoneurones of the thoracic spinal cord. Progress Brain Research. 1964; 12: 259-73.

Singer R. Estimation of age from cranial suture closure: report on its unreliability. Journal of Forensic Medicine. 1953;1: 52-59.

Steenvoorden GP, van de Velde JP, Prahl-Anderson B. The effect of duration and magnitude of tensile mechanical forces on sutural tissue in vivo. European Journal of Orthodontics. 1990; 12(3): 330-339.

Sutherland WG. The cranial bowl. 1st ed. Minnesota: W. G. Sutherland; 1939.

Todd TW, Lyon DW Jr. Endocranial suture closure: its progress and age relationship. Part I: adult males of white stock. Am J Phys Anthrop. 1924; VII (3): 325-384.

Upledger JE & Vredevoogd JD. Craniosacral Therapy. Illinois: Eastland Press; 1983.

Vleming A, Mooney V., Snijders C, Dorman T. Low back pain and its relation to the sacroiliac joint. California; 1992.

Wallace W et al. Ultrasonic measurement of intracranial pulsation at 9 cycles per minutes. Journal of Neurology. Reprint.

Wood J. Dynamic response of human cranial bones. J. Biomech. 1971; 4:1-12.

World Health Organization (WHO), Media Centre, Headache Disorders, http://www.who.int/mediacentre/factsheets/fs277/en/.

Zanakis MF, Dimeo J, Madonna S, Morgan M, Dasby E. Objective measurement of the CRI with manipulation and palpation of the sacrum. JAOA. 1996; 96:101-9.

About the Author

Dr. Joseph Unger Jr. completed his premedical studies at the University of Missouri – Columbia, majoring in zoology and psychology. Following a year of self-study in healthcare alternatives, he entered Logan University's College of Chiropractic graduating in 1979. He has been a practicing chiropractic physician since that time.

Dr. Unger began studying the Sacro Occipital Technic™ Methods of chiropractic and Chiropractic Craniopathy with Dr. Major Bertrand De Jarnette in 1975 while still a student. He began teaching for Dr. De Jarnette in 1979 and has been an instructor at Logan University since 1984. His taught these techniques worldwide and presented his research findings at various conferences. Currently he is immediate past president of SORSI and has been active in that organization since taking his first classes with Dr. De Jarnette.

Dr. Unger is also published, *Neurological Reflex First Aid*, a self-help book based on the research and teachings of Dr. De Jarnette and the principles of SOT®.

Index

A

AlphaBio Centrix xii, 85, 163, 167, 170
Anatomists New Tools 30
arachnoid mater 25
Attention Deficit Disorder (ADD) xiv, 143
Attention Deficit Hyperactivity Disorder (ADHD) xiv, 143
Autoimmune Dysfunction 161, 184, 185, 188

B

Blood Brain Barrier (BBB) xi

C

Candida 165, 166
Category I 16, 198, 229
Category II xvii, 6, 7, 16, 20, 21, 22, 33, 38, 41, 45, 46, 47, 49, 51, 52, 53, 54,
        57, 59, 60, 64, 65, 67, 69, 70, 71, 73, 89, 97, 103, 104, 105, 109, 110, 113,
        114, 115, 116, 118, 119, 122, 127, 128, 132, 133, 145, 146, 157, 158, 159,
        163, 191, 193, 198, 199, 215, 216, 217, 219, 220, 225, 226, 229, 231
Category III 16, 105, 157, 158, 159, 163, 229
Category II subluxation complex 6, 7, 21, 22, 33, 41, 45, 46, 47, 49, 51, 52, 53,
        57, 59, 60, 64, 67, 69, 70, 73, 97, 113, 114, 115, 119, 122, 127, 128, 133,
        145, 146, 157, 158, 191, 193, 217, 225, 231
cerebral spinal fluid (CSF) xiii, 103, 229, 230
cerebral vascular accident 83
Certified Craniopath 17, 104, 105, 122, 141, 227, 229, 231
cervical spine 34, 37, 64, 65, 154
Chelation therapy 162, 180
Chiropractic Craniopathy xii, xiv, xv, xvii, 2, 8, 13, 15, 22, 49, 65, 67, 78, 81,
        85, 89, 91, 92, 103, 111, 113, 116, 194, 198, 199, 221, 230, 231, 232, 233,
        241
chiropractic physician 13, 14, 17, 21, 31, 44, 70, 87, 97, 119, 221, 231, 232, 241

Clinical Purification 174
Colon Cleansing 179
concussion 74, 77, 78, 142
condyle 56, 58, 62, 63, 225
Cottam, Dr. Nephi xiv, 13, 197
cranial bones xiii, xiv, 14, 19, 20, 22, 33, 60, 71, 72, 136, 165, 229, 232, 234, 235, 238, 240
cranial distortion 64, 89, 90, 93, 95, 174, 192, 226
cranial meninges 25
cranial nerves 27, 60, 71, 72, 73
cranial osteopathy xiv, 15, 221
Cranial Sacral Respiratory Mechanism (CSRM) 22, 230
cranial subluxations 7, 16, 22, 23, 24, 76, 91, 93, 104, 114, 119, 124, 143, 144, 233
Craniosacral Therapy (CST) 116
CST 15, 116, 227, 230, 231

D

DCS 6, 20, 22, 36, 71, 73, 103, 135, 149, 191, 194, 199, 231, 234
De Jarnette Cranial Syndrome (DCS) 6, 20, 22, 36, 71, 73, 103, 135, 149, 191, 194, 199, 231, 234
De Jarnette, Dr. Major Bertrand xiv, 6, 14, 15, 29, 195, 233, 241
dementia xi, xiv
detoxification 156, 159, 162, 173, 174, 175, 176, 177, 178, 179, 181
DICS 17, 215, 216, 227, 231, 232
dural sleeves 37
dura mater 25, 26, 41, 77, 229
dynamometer 115

E

EDTA 180, 181
EEG 113
energy healing patches 85
Ennis, Dr. Dennis 152, 190
Extremity System 16

F

fasting 176, 178
Fellow of the International Craniopathic Society (FICS) 232
Fibromyalgia xvii, 155, 156, 157, 158, 159, 160, 227, 238
football 78, 79, 80
frontal bones 19

G

Georges Lakhovsky 168
Grinder, John 109

H

headaches 5, 28, 29, 30, 31, 32, 54, 69, 77, 79, 81, 92, 93, 94, 131, 132, 133, 134, 142, 152, 156
head trauma xiv, 1, 101, 141
Hippocrates xiii, 13
homunculus 159
Hospers, Lasca 113
Howat, Dr. Jonathan 90
hypermobile SIJ 52

I

Ilium 20, 53, 55, 57, 59, 62, 225, 232
Infrared Sauna 178
innate energy 3
Integrated Sutural Protocols xiv, 20, 104, 133, 226, 234
International Craniopathic Society 17, 227, 231, 232

K

kinesiology 114

L

law of reciprocal relationships 20
Logan College of Chiropractic 40, 190, 197, 219
Logan, Dr. Hugh B. 40

Logan University 40, 41, 117, 121, 151, 152, 241
low back pain 5, 45, 46, 54, 68, 69, 70, 99, 145, 146, 148, 191

M

mandible 56, 58, 234
multiple sclerosis xiv, 67, 103

N

Nordenstrom, Bjorn E. W. 3
nutritional deficiencies 29, 92, 152

O

Occipital Fibers xvii, 28, 151, 153
occipital fiber system 28, 31, 32, 154
occiput 19, 21, 31, 35, 55, 60, 65, 229, 232

P

Pain Control 16
Palmer, Dr. David D. 3
Parkinson's disease xi
pia mater 25
plantar fasciitis 68, 70, 140, 141
Primary Respiratory Mechanism 14, 33, 233
proprioception 104, 105, 136
Protomorphogen (PMG) Therapy 183

R

Raw Foods 181
reductionist theory 3, 4
Rife, Dr. Royal 167

S

Sacroiliac Joint (SIJ) 51
Sacro Occipital Research Society International, Inc. (SORSI) 156, 195, 233
Sacro Occipital Technic™ (SOT®) xiv, 15, 233

sacrum 20, 21, 26, 34, 35, 37, 40, 51, 55, 65, 124, 160, 229, 232, 233, 234, 239, 240
SI belt 45, 46, 47
sphenoid 19, 137
spinal cord 33, 35, 39, 101, 236, 238, 240
spinal nerves 27, 70
Split Face Technique 121
stroke 81, 82, 83, 85, 86, 189, 195
subarachnoid space 25, 33
subluxation 6, 7, 20, 21, 22, 23, 33, 39, 41, 45, 46, 47, 49, 51, 52, 53, 57, 59, 60, 62, 64, 65, 67, 69, 70, 71, 73, 93, 97, 113, 114, 115, 116, 119, 122, 127, 128, 132, 133, 135, 136, 137, 138, 139, 140, 141, 145, 146, 157, 158, 165, 191, 193, 217, 225, 230, 231, 234
Suboccipital Fiber System 16
Sutherland, Dr. William Garner 14
sutures 19, 71, 73, 74, 77, 89, 135, 204, 209, 237, 238, 239
Swedenborg, Emmanuel xiii, 14

T

Technic 17, 18, 31, 65, 194, 198, 213, 215, 227, 236
temporal bone 20, 21, 54, 55, 56, 57, 58, 59, 61, 62, 135, 136, 146, 225, 234
Temporal mandibular dysfunction (TMD) 234
Temporal mandibular joint (TMJ) 234
The Science of Chiropractic 39
Trapezius Fiber System 16
Traumatic Brain Injury (TBI) 77, 103, 234
trigeminal neuralgia 72

V

Ventricles 234
Vital Force 3
Vitalistic Healing 3, 4

Made in the
USA
Lexington, KY